AN EDUCATOR'S GUIDE TO UNIVERSITY APPLICATIONS

WENDY HEYDORN AND
LAURENCE GOODWIN

trotman t

An Educator's Guide to University Applications

This first edition published in 2025 by Trotman, an imprint of Trotman Indigo Publishing Ltd, 18e Charles Street, Bath BA1 1HX

© Trotman Indigo Publishing Ltd 2025

Authors: Wendy Heydorn and Laurence Goodwin

British Library Cataloguing in Publication Data
A catalogue record for this book is available from the British Library.

Paperback ISBN 978 1 911724 51 3
eISBN 978 1 911724 52 0

All rights reserved. This book is sold subject to the condition that it shall not, by way of trade or otherwise, be lent, resold, hired out or otherwise circulated without the publisher's prior written consent in any form of binding or cover other than that in which it is published and without a similar condition including this condition being imposed on the subsequent purchaser. No part of this publication may be reproduced, stored in a retrieval system or transmitted in any form or by any means, electronic and mechanical, photocopying, recording or otherwise without prior permission of Trotman Indigo Publishing.

Every effort has been made to trace copyright holders and to obtain their permission for the use of copyright material. The publisher apologises for any errors or omissions, and would be grateful to be notified of any corrections that should be incorporated in future editions of this book.

The views expressed in this publication are those of the authors and do not reflect the official stance of their past, present or future employers.

The authorised representative in the EEA is Easy Access System Europe Oü (EAS), Mustamäe tee 50, 10621 Tallinn, Estonia.

Printed and bound in the UK by 4edge Ltd, Hockley, Essex.

All details in this book were correct at the time of going to press. To keep up to date with all the latest news and updates and to access the online resources that accompany this book, use this QR code or visit www.trotman.co.uk/pages/an-educators-guide-to-university-applications-resources.

Contents

About the authors — v
Acknowledgements — vii
Preface — ix
Introduction — 1

1| Understanding the options for students beyond school or college — 3
2| How to increase students' chances of success — 23
3| Understanding perspectives and voices — 41
4| How to structure support based on time and staff availability — 57
5| Managing university applications: UK focus — 83
6| Supporting personal statements: UCAS focus — 115
7| Writing university references: UCAS focus — 127
8| Managing university applications: US and international university focus — 145
9| Writing university references and supporting application essays: US focus — 175
10| Communication with students and staff — 189
11| Managing expectations — 197
12| The role of AI in university applications — 211
Conclusion — 221

About the authors

Wendy Heydorn is Director of Higher Education at Sevenoaks School. Having graduated from Fitzwilliam College, Cambridge, she went on to study for an MA at King's College London and a PGCE. She has co-authored three Theory of Knowledge textbooks, including *Theory of Knowledge for the IB Diploma Course Guide* (2020). She has expertise in Higher Education advice for students aged 16–18 and the management of university applications and volunteered for four years on the Secondary Education Advisory Group (SEAG) at UCAS. Having worked in the educational sector as a teacher of Theory of Knowledge, Head of Religious Studies and Sixth Form Tutor, she is committed to offering students the best possible preparation for university, the workplace and beyond.

Laurence Goodwin is Head of US and International University Applications at Sevenoaks School. She is a specialist in advising students and managing university applications. Educated in the US and with degrees from St. Andrews, the Courtauld Institute of Art and a PGCE from King's College London, she has experience with school and university systems on both sides of the Atlantic. As a trained teacher, Laurence has taught Latin and drama and worked as a University Adviser at schools in Oxford, Gloucestershire and on the Isle of Wight. Prior to taking on her role at Sevenoaks, Laurence has been a Head of Department, Sixth Form Tutor and Head of EPQ. Laurence is a member of IACAC (International Association for College Admission Counseling) and chairs the London Schools University Counsellor Network. She is currently studying for an MSc in Learning and Teaching at the University of Oxford.

Acknowledgements

We would like to thank the Higher Education Advisers and school counsellors with whom we've collaborated over the years, as well as all the Admissions Officers and tutors at universities in the UK and further afield. We'd also like to thank our colleagues for their support, and especially those who have generously taken the time to give us feedback on various chapters: Jane Alexander Orr, Julia Kiggell, Graham Lacey, Kim Nicholas and Jamie Potton. A particularly big thank you to Gill Shukla who read the whole first draft and to Emily Wright, Technology Degree Apprentice at Morgan Stanley, for her contribution on Degree Apprenticeships in Chapters 1 and 2. We are grateful to our former colleagues, Katy Ricks and the late Ruth Greenhalgh, for their legacy and leadership and to our current colleagues for their collaboration: Jesse Elzinga, Charlotte Glanville, Julia Barnes and Giuliana Brooks. We'd also like to thank our parents and families for their patience and support. Wendy is grateful to her parents, Judy and Geoff Worham, who both went to university as mature students while she was growing up and inspired her to read and think. Finally, we'd like to thank Nicola Cattini, Alexandra Price and Louisa Smith at Trotman for their expertise and for helping us to share our insights and experience with a wider audience.

Preface

Schools and colleges can have widely varying priorities, strengths and stresses, not to mention legal requirements. If you are in Scotland, Wales or Northern Ireland, there may be country-specific legislation you need to consider. While our experience comes from working within the independent sector in England, the principles under which we operate – that all students need support in making crucial decisions about their futures – are applicable to all settings. Careers and university guidance can often be an afterthought or tacked on to someone's 'real' job regardless of what type of school in which you are working. This shouldn't be the case.

There are many types of educational institutions in the UK educating 16- to 18-year-olds: state secondary schools, academies, comprehensives, further education colleges, grammar schools, independent day and boarding schools, special schools, city technology colleges, overseas schools, Sixth Form colleges, pupil referral units and tertiary colleges.

We assume throughout that your students will apply to undergraduate courses taught in English in the UK, US or elsewhere. If your students are applying for courses not taught in English, you may need to adjust your approach. This book is written for staff and educators working in various settings rather than students or parents; most of the material is equally relevant to UK and international (non-UK) students applying to UK universities, as well as for all students applying to universities outside the UK.

Who is this book for?

The idea for this book came from the emails and conversations we both had with colleagues who have been tasked with managing their school's careers or university admissions programme. We realised through these interactions that while there is a plethora of guidance on how to set up and run careers departments in schools, the same information was not readily available for teachers and staff managing university applications. The information we provide here will be most relevant for colleagues in British and international schools in the UK who are educating 16- to 18-year-olds. Our aim is to share our understanding of good practice with teachers, Tutors, Heads of Sixth Form, Headteachers and Advisers from schools and post-16 colleges,

Careers Advisers and Heads of Student Services for the benefit of the students in our care.

So, if you are reading this book, we assume you are involved in careers or university guidance. Perhaps you applied for the role, or maybe the responsibility was given to you because you have a gap in your timetable. You might be thinking, 'I'm up for a challenge', or you may feel daunted at the prospect. Perhaps you're not sure how you're meant to add something else to your long 'to-do' list, especially something that you know is very important to your students. Equally, you may be an experienced Head of Sixth Form, or leader of a Higher Education or Careers department looking to expand your provision or reconsider what you offer to your students. We hope this book is relevant for all colleagues, wherever you are in your professional journey.

All students, regardless of their school, background or other factors, should have access to the full range of educational, training or employment opportunities available after they leave school or college. You are a very important part of helping them access the information they need to make informed decisions; never underestimate the power your role has to actually change and benefit a student's life.

Careers guidance and HE advice

There is an important and very valuable distinction between 'Careers Guidance' and 'Higher Education advice'. This book focuses on the latter: university admissions and supporting students' university applications. This is where we have the most experience and where we think we can make a difference to you, our colleagues in other schools. This book is focused on managing university applications, so while we make reference to vocational pathways, employment and training, these are not detailed as extensively in this book, though we do recognise that for many students, university will not be the right option, and you may have to act as both a University Adviser *and* Careers Adviser. For more detail on managing Careers programmes, we recommend starting with *The Careers Leader Handbook* by David Andrews and Tristram Hooley, also published by Trotman (third edition 2025), and the Career Development Institute: https://www.thecdi.net/

Supporting students with their post-18 options

We set out the details of our applications support provision in Chapter 4 as an example of how you could organise your own; however, we recognise that what works in one setting may not work in yours or that your resourcing may not (yet) allow you to manage applications as suggested here. We hope that seeing some options will help you to decide what is right for your setting and to advocate for yourself with your leadership if you need more support.

Our strategy has taken many years to develop and embed in our school and is the culmination of the work of colleagues who went before us and the input of colleagues we work with now. It takes time for schools to get staffing just right, to gain the trust and support of students and parents, to collaborate with governors and to build your contacts in the university sector.

How to read this book

In each chapter, we have provided general guidance, practical ideas and scenarios that you may encounter when working with students, other members of staff and parents. The guidance is intended as a starting point for your own plan and will hopefully give you a sense of what needs to be considered when dealing with each aspect of the university application process. The scenarios included reflect a range of possible situations and issues arising in schools and colleges; you will likely find that some are more relevant to you than others. These are generic scenarios intended for reflection and discussion and are not specific to any particular school or college setting.

Online resources

This book is accompanied by various online resources, including templates, FAQs and timelines for staff and students, which you can download via the QR code and/or web link at the start of this book.

Introduction

Careers Education, Information, Advice and Guidance (CEIAG) is a broad and important area in all schools and colleges that encompasses the more specialised area of university advising. In this book, we've tried to suggest different approaches to the basics of university advising and offer some of the questions and scenarios that might arise in the course of your work, which we hope will give you a touch point for dealing with related or similar issues in your own setting. The book features include 'plans and timelines' and 'scenarios', which are intended as starting points only; your particular students' needs and interests may influence what you choose to do at specific times over the course of their time at school. We've also included ways to build and strengthen your approach to managing applications when you have the time and resources to do so. Keep what works for you and discard the rest; the most important thing is that your CEIAG programme serves and empowers your students to make good decisions about their futures.

And yet, careers and university advice is not always prioritised in schools. In some settings, this is due to severe financial constraints, but in others, it is simply a lack of understanding on the part of leadership as to the importance of creating and resourcing a robust programme. Recent initiatives, such as the growth of widening participation at UK universities and recent legislation enacted by Parliament, have brought the importance of Careers guidance and access to universities to the fore of the national discussion in Britain. Regardless of the type of school or college, CEIAG must be a priority, and it may fall to you to ensure that your school leaders and governors understand the latest statutory requirements.

Working with young people

Students can apply for jobs, apprenticeships or to universities anywhere in the world. We hope that the information in this book will help you understand what you need to do to support students and advocate for the resources and time that you need.

In addition, issues with mental health and the cost of living make this a difficult time for many young people. Furthermore, the impact of AI and automation of jobs and the limited number of jobs and graduate roles make this a difficult landscape to navigate. Nevertheless, we have an opportunity to help young people think positively about their futures.

Schools and colleges have an obligation to provide career advice and support to students, but every educational setting is unique, with its own constraints, finite resources, trends, precedents and expectations. This makes giving advice on how to create, manage and maintain a programme of support tricky, as there are so many factors that need to be taken into account. Start from the key principle that every student needs and deserves knowledgeable, impartial student-centred advice when considering their future. Everything should follow from there.

1 | Understanding the options for students beyond school or college

In 2014, Sir John Holman outlined the eight benchmarks for Careers guidance in a report published by the Gatsby Charitable Foundation; these benchmarks are known as the Gatsby Benchmarks and form the basis for CEIAG. In 2018, the government issued guidance directing schools to have a named Careers Leader; since then, schools and colleges have spent considerable time, expertise and resources on improving the quality of their Careers guidance. Gatsby Benchmark 7 requires schools to develop encounters with further and Higher Education and the workplace; students need to become aware of a variety of technical, vocational, educational and academic routes.

Increasingly, students want to make multiple applications to maximise all of their options, so it's not unusual to support a student who is applying to Degree Apprenticeships in the UK, as well as applying via UCAS to UK universities and for scholarships at US universities. Chapter 1 is intended to increase awareness of the options for students.

This chapter will cover:

- school requirements and the duty of schools and colleges to support CEIAG;
- the updated Gatsby Benchmarks based on the 2024 report 'Good Careers Guidance: The Next 10 Years' published by the Gatsby Charitable Foundation;
- the options for school leavers at 18+ and how to support these students;
- an outline of various post-18+ options in order to help you encourage students to make informed decisions, including education, training and employment.

School requirements

Consider what your legal and educational obligations are. Depending on the context and possibly the country you are in, there may be specific legal requirements that you must ensure you meet. In the United Kingdom, for example, maintained schools and academies in England must refer to Section 45A of the Education Act 1997 in considering how students engage with Careers guidance. Schools and colleges have a duty to provide CEIAG to students in Years 7–13. Schools and colleges are supported by the Careers and Enterprise Company (CEC), and the quality of CEIAG is inspected by Ofsted.

- Schools and colleges need to measure the impact of their Careers provision and their success in meeting all of the Gatsby Benchmarks, which form part of the guidance to schools on CEIAG provided by the Department for Education.
- Compass+, is a tool provided by the Careers and Enterprise Company (available to eligible schools) that measures the impact of Careers provision in your educational setting.
- It is important to stay up to date with changes and ensure that your school or college is compliant with the statutory requirements for CEIAG. For example, a House of Commons Committee report, entitled 'Careers Education, Information, Advice and Guidance', published on 29 June 2023, made recommendations to the government, which could result in changes to statutory guidance in due course.
- Provider Access Legislation (PAL) is the latest version of the Baker Clause, which states that schools must allow colleges and training providers access to every student in Years 8–13 to discuss non-academic routes such as apprenticeships and T levels. This means that schools must organise at least six encounters with training providers from Year 8 to Year 13.
- All educators in schools and colleges have a responsibility to minimise the risk of young people becoming NEET (not in education, employment or training), and this chapter aims to inspire staff who can encourage young people to recognise their post-18 opportunities and make the most of their potential.

Gatsby benchmarks

The Department for Education states: '*The provider access legislation (occasionally referred to as the "Baker Clause") requires all schools and academies to provide opportunities for a range of education and training providers to access all Year 8 to 13 pupils to inform them about approved technical education qualifications and apprenticeships. Through the Skills and Post-16 Act 2022, the government has strengthened this legislation by introducing a minimum number of six provider encounters that every school must provide and, for the first time, introduces parameters around the duration and content of these encounters so that we can ensure they are of high quality . . . To support this, the department is funding The Careers & Enterprise Company to support schools and colleges to develop Careers programmes in line with their careers requirements and the Gatsby Benchmarks.*' https://assets.publishing.service.gov.uk/media/63b69f3fe90e077246c83323/Careers_guidance_and_access_for_education_and_training_providers_.pdf

The Gatsby Benchmarks were introduced to give schools a framework that would help them meet their statutory obligations with regard to career and post-education options advice. In 2024, the Gatsby Foundation released an updated set of benchmarks reflecting changes in technology, education and the labour market since the benchmarks were first introduced over 10 years ago. Schools in England are expected to implement the revised Gatsby Benchmarks by September 2025. Each of these has implications for senior leaders in schools and colleges:

- careers at the heart of education and leadership;
- inclusion and impact for each and every young person;
- meaningful and varied encounters and experiences;
- focusing on the use of information and data;
- engagements of parents and carers.

Useful link

- https://www.gatsbybenchmarks.org.uk/app/uploads/2024/11/good-career-guidance-the-next-10-years-report.pdf

> **QUESTIONS TO CONSIDER**
>
> - What evidence do you have that you are addressing the various Gatsby Benchmarks?
> - What does your Compass+ data show?
> - How can you make the best use of this tool and other tools and resources provided by the Careers and Enterprise Company?
> - How does your school or college prepare students for university or work beyond school?
> - What can you and other colleagues do to support every student and raise their awareness of all their options?
> - Who comes into your school to talk about these opportunities? For example, employers, colleges and university representatives, or past students?
> - How aware are your students of the different routes into education, training and employment?

The options available to students and approaches needed to support these students

There are so many possibilities and options available to students, including university, specialist colleges and the workplace. Some students might decide to go straight into employment. The appeal may be the prospect of earning money, studying alongside working and the lure of some amount of financial independence. Their need to earn money may be due to personal or family circumstances or their responsibility to contribute to costs at home. In short, paid work may be a necessity or it may be a genuine choice. Students should be earning the minimum wage but should be wary of zero-hours contracts.

An overview of post-18+ options

It is important that students have accurate and up-to-date information and advice about different qualifications and training options. On the following pages are some examples of different routes beyond school into education, training or employment. However, there are routes we don't have space to cover here. The list here is not exhaustive, but it is intended to get you thinking about how you will gather, promote and share this information (or any other appropriate opportunities or routes) in your educational context:

1. Apprenticeships;
2. Degree Apprenticeships;
3. Higher Technical Qualifications (HTQs);
4. Foundation courses;
5. Art Foundation courses;
6. Foundation degrees;
7. Conservatoires for the performing arts;
8. BTEC Higher Nationals and BTEC Higher Apprenticeships;
9. Degree courses at UK universities;
10. Degree courses at US and international universities;
11. Gap Years and post-qualification applications;
12. Access to Higher Education courses;
13. Setting up a business, enterprise or other entrepreneurial activities.

> **QUESTIONS TO CONSIDER**
>
> - How might you encourage students to weigh the pros and cons of these different post-18+ options, in terms of the potential benefits, opportunities, costs and suitability?

1. Apprenticeships

There is so much momentum behind apprenticeships, as well as a shift towards many students considering them alongside traditional university degrees as a potential post-18 option. During an apprenticeship, students will do paid work and train to gain a qualification. Employers select candidates directly, so students need to navigate the selection process and impress the employer to get hired. Adverts for apprenticeship vacancies are 'live' for a limited time, so students need to be proactive and act fast when the application window opens. There are various types, including:

- Traineeships (Level 1 or Level 2, lasting up to 6 months, unpaid but providing skills and qualifications);
- Intermediate (Level 2, equivalent to 5 GCSEs);
- Advanced (Level 3, equivalent to 2 A levels);
- Higher (Level 4 and above, equivalent to Foundation degrees and above);
- Degree Apprenticeships: combining paid employment with university study (Level 6 or 7).

2. Degree Apprenticeships

In the current cost-of-living crisis, the opportunities and benefits of gaining a degree with no debt are likely to mean that Degree Apprenticeships remain a popular option. Degree Apprenticeships (Level 6 or Level 7) offer the opportunity to work while studying for a degree, with tuition fees covered by the employer. Degree Apprenticeships are a prestigious option. For example, you can become a solicitor via an apprenticeship, a job that in the past required a traditional university degree. From September 2024, it became possible to qualify as a doctor via an apprenticeship route.

Unlike university, where students typically take out loans to pay for their tuition fees, with Degree Apprenticeships, the employer pays for a student's tuition fees and pays them a salary straight away. Apprenticeships typically involve approximately 80% of learning on the job and 20% studying. Some apprentices go to work four days a week and college one day, while others work most of the year and study for a couple of months.

Apprenticeships can be an entry into various technical professions such as engineering (e.g. Rolls Royce and Jaguar Land Rover) and financial services (such as JP Morgan, Goldman Sachs and Morgan Stanley). However, apprenticeships offer routes into every industry, from health and social care to construction to hospitality. Students apply directly to the employer, for example, the BBC, the Civil Service, MI5 and MI6.

However, a Degree Apprenticeship isn't an easy option, but everything points to it bringing long-term career benefits to students who embark upon this route. Increasingly, a Degree Apprenticeship is an elite pathway. These are prestigious opportunities and highly competitive; the 'top students' in your setting may prefer to apply for apprenticeships either alongside their UCAS choices or instead of a traditional UCAS university application. The level of competition, based on the high ratio of applicants to places, can be more intense than at highly selective universities such as the University of Oxford or the University of Cambridge and even more competitive than some of the top US universities. The benefits are enormous: students graduate with no debt and are likely to have secure employment afterwards. However, from the viewpoint of a school or college, these applications can be difficult to manage and track in large numbers.

- Applications are made directly to an employer in multiple career areas.
- The selection process, timelines and deadlines all vary.
- The job advert may 'go live' and then close.
- References or documents may be required with little notice.

1| Understanding the Options for Students beyond School or College

- It is challenging to track these students and the progress of these applications through the various elements of an employer's selection process.
- Students may ask for help, such as interview practice, and be given very little notice to prepare before their real interview.

They need to be highly organised individuals, especially if they are also applying through UCAS. Students need to be proactive and search for these opportunities. Staff should consider how they will promote these opportunities, help prepare students for the competitive process and provide documents and references as needed. However, consider carefully how you will promote these opportunities, as international students studying in UK schools and colleges may not be eligible for Degree Apprenticeships.

Case study: Part 1

In this two-part case study, we invited Emily Wright, a technology degree apprentice at Morgan Stanley. We asked her to respond to a number of questions, followed by an overview of the selection process, which you can find at the end of Chapter 2. Emily was a Year 13 International Baccalaureate Diploma Programme student when she applied for multiple Degree Apprenticeships, and she received offers from Morgan Stanley and UBS. At the same time, she also applied to various UK universities via UCAS. We are grateful to Emily for her valuable insights here and for providing the following responses to our questions:

1. What was the preparation needed for your Degree Apprenticeship applications, for example, CV, covering letter, work experience, super-curricular activities, reading or other elements?
   - I made a CV in Year 11 and updated it in Year 12 and Year 13, following a template online, and I looked at a range of CV examples.
   - Covering letters are needed for almost all Degree Apprenticeships, and I wrote them individually for each company I applied to.
2. Was there anything you did at school or in your International Baccalaureate Diploma Programme curriculum that helped you succeed?
   - The IB Diploma curriculum helped me prepare for the application process, as I was familiar with writing essays and giving presentations. I also had a broad range of subject knowledge that I could call upon at various different points in the selection and interview process.

- Volunteering is a massive plus for many of the big firms. Companies might be actively looking for students who have added value to a community or taken part in a range of activities outside the classroom, so doing volunteering at school outside of school time helped my applications.
- Languages are also loved by all global firms I applied to – most people in my apprentice cohort are bilingual, and a number of them speak four or five languages.
- The sort of thinking and discussion in IB Theory of Knowledge helped a lot more than I thought it would, so I would recommend anyone considering applying to improve on their critical thinking skills in Year 12 before applications start.

3. How did you manage your applications alongside your schoolwork and your UCAS applications?
   - I found balancing everything very manageable, but I recognise I am reasonably good at time management. I think it's a good idea to write down the dates applications open and apply within two days otherwise, it may be too late at big firms who might close their applications early.
   - I didn't spend much time on UCAS applications at all; most of my time was spent on my Degree Apprenticeship applications before the Year 12 exam revision became a priority. A top tip is to prepare everything so it's ready to go in Year 12 or the summer, as then it will be a quicker process.

4. Do you have any practical tips for applicants?
   - I made a notes page on each company before the video interviews.
   - Don't worry about interviews; just speak as if you're speaking with a teacher at school – not too informal but definitely not too formal.
   - The company chooses you for not just your skill set but also for your personality and authenticity, so if you do get an offer, don't worry whether it's the right fit for you or not – it will be.

5. Can you elaborate on the skills needed at each stage – to prepare, to apply and to succeed on a Degree Apprenticeship?
   - Examples of soft skills during a Degree Apprenticeship application:
     - Time management;
     - Confidence in interviews;
     - Leadership and teamwork.

(Sidenote: some companies prefer those who are the loudest in the interviews; some prefer either a quieter leader or team player – don't do what doesn't feel comfortable, but do make sure you bring up new ideas and have a voice.)
- Examples of soft skills during a Degree Apprenticeship:
  - Time management;
  - Networking skills;
  - Confidence (this is number one without a doubt);
  - Efficiency.

6. What are the benefits of pursuing a Degree Apprenticeship? How did you decide between your offers from Morgan Stanley, UBS and your university offers from the University of Exeter, University of Bath and Imperial College London?
   - I always wanted a Degree Apprenticeship over a university place. My preference has always been to learn on the job *vs.* in lectures.
   - Money shouldn't be the deciding factor, but it is definitely a consideration.
   - I chose Morgan Stanley as the university (Queen Mary, London) was in-person; there was a rotation each year, allowing me to experience different teams and meet new people. The culture of the firm was also a key factor.
   - Another benefit is you start building a professional network from age 18, which you don't realise is a massive benefit until you get there.
   - The networks and social life are really good, better than university, I would say. There is something going on every week and loads of opportunities to socialise in different situations and form good friendships.

7. Do you have any reflections on your first few weeks and months as an apprentice, and what are your thoughts on the transition from school to the workplace, the other degree apprentices, and what it's like in your new role?
   - I've loved it so far and have no regrets. I didn't find the transition too challenging, but it is very different from a school environment and something I had never experienced before.
   - I've been focused on building my professional network and meeting people high up in the firm, both in technology and business/finance.
   - The university part at Queen Mary (one day a week) is a good way to meet other degree apprentices, for example, apprentices from Goldman Sachs and Amazon.

- My role is intense due to the amount of information I have to learn. I've had to learn three different coding languages from scratch, which has been hard, but now I'm at the stage where I'm doing the same work as the team and can mostly do everything independently.
- The support at Morgan Stanley is amazing, with a mentor, team buddy, apprentice buddy, career manager, business mentor and manager, just to name a few.
- The first few weeks of the apprenticeship may be harder than the International Baccalaureate Diploma Programme in terms of the amount you're learning and time management. If students are struggling with sticking to deadlines in IB or are having a hard time with coursework and independence in Sixth Form, Degree Apprenticeships probably aren't the best route to take, as the learning curve is near vertical.

PRACTICAL TOOLS AND TIPS

Check dates of Apprenticeship Fairs in your area and accompany students to the event. The students will have a better idea of what the employers are looking for and the level of competition. Consider how you can help students prepare for the following:

- Research into the Degree Apprenticeships available;
- Producing a CV and covering letter;
- Assessment centres;
- Interviews.

https://www.apprenticeships.gov.uk/apprentices/preparing-apprenticeship

3. Higher Technical Qualifications

Students can go on to study for an HTQ. Examples of these Level 4 and 5 courses are the Higher National Certificate and Higher National Diploma, Foundation Degrees and Higher Education Diplomas, which offer work-related courses. An HNC (Higher National Certificate) is equivalent to the first year of a university degree, and an HND (Higher National Diploma) is equivalent to the first two years. These are either one- or two-year courses approved by employers, and students can search for them on UCAS. These can lead to a full bachelor's degree and are an alternative to apprenticeships. They are offered by FE colleges and universities in a range of areas, from Construction to Health and Science; Business and Administration; Education and early years; Engineering and Manufacturing; and Legal, Finance and Accounting.

From September 2025, there will be more areas available, including agriculture, environmental and animal care; catering and hospitality; creative and design; care services; protective services; and sales, marketing and procurement.

4. Foundation courses

For students who want to study engineering at university but don't have the level of Maths and Science required, a Foundation year is a possible route. Also known as a 'Year Zero', these are suitable for students who either don't have the grades or the required subjects to enter straight into a degree course. Universities offer Foundation years with the expectation that some students will progress onto a full degree course. For example:

https://www.uea.ac.uk/study/information-for/foundation-year

For example, the University of Cambridge offers an excellent arts and humanities Foundation year for students who have experienced educational disadvantage; not all students progress to a full degree at Cambridge, but a significant number will.

https://www.undergraduate.study.cam.ac.uk/courses/foundation-year

Similarly, the University of Oxford has a one-year Foundation degree programme for students interested in progressing to study Classics, English or Theology and Religion. Students who complete the year are awarded a Certificate in Higher Education (CertHE) qualification.

https://www.ox.ac.uk/admissions/undergraduate/courses/course-listing/fyhumanities

5. Art Foundation courses

These are Art and Design courses for students who want to study this subject at university. Some university Art courses require a Foundation year, and the applications are either direct to the art school or sometimes via UCAS, depending on the degree course. Art Foundation courses are also available at FE colleges, and there are no fees for under-19s, for example: https://www.northkent.ac.uk/courses/creative-media/foundation-diploma-in-art-design-tv-film-digital-journalism-level-4-dartford

There are also performing arts Foundation courses, sometimes offered to students who are unsuccessful in their degree course applications.

6. Foundation degrees

Foundation degrees are a stand-alone qualification that is equivalent to two-thirds of a bachelor's degree. They combine academic and workplace skills and generally focus on a specific workplace or profession. https://www.ucas.com/undergraduate/what-and-where-study/choosing-course/foundation-degrees

7. Conservatoires for the performing arts

The performing arts are a fantastic option for some students: conservatoires for music, drama or dance school. An application to one of these conservatoires can be either in addition to a UCAS application or instead of one. For example, a student could apply for English and acting at the University of Warwick via UCAS and also apply directly through UCAS conservatoires for courses at any one of the following UK conservatoires:

- Royal Birmingham Conservatoire;
- LAMDA;
- Leeds Conservatoire;
- Royal Academy of Music;
- Royal College of Music;
- Royal Northern College of Music;
- Royal Conservatoire of Scotland;
- Royal Welsh College of Music and Drama;
- Trinity Laban Conservatoire of Music and Dance.

Typically, they will need an academic reference and a practical reference written by a music teacher or drama teacher. This is a difficult area to track and manage, given that there is no place on UCAS to identify or record who is making an application via UCAS conservatoires. Auditions are usually a key feature in the selection process.

Consider how you will track and manage conservatoires applications, and ensure that you have the academic and practical references needed by the deadlines. Discuss with the student who can provide their practical reference and maybe produce a reference guide for these staff or share the relevant links and instructions.

UCAS conservatoires: https://www.ucas.com/conservatoires/studying-conservatoire/thinking-about-performing-arts

8. BTEC Higher Nationals and BTEC Higher Apprenticeships

BTEC offers a fantastic route for students who might want to progress to university or another Higher Education institution but may also want to study locally while living at home. Some BTEC qualifications are being phased out if they overlap with T level provision, so students need to check with institutions. Schools, Sixth Form colleges and further education colleges offer a range of BTEC courses, for example, in IT, health and social care, beauty, business or media. BTEC Higher Nationals comprise:

- Higher National Certificates (HNCs/Level 4), which are equivalent to the first year of university and are also available as part-time (two years) and online courses;
- Higher National Diplomas (HNDs/Level 5), which are equivalent to the first two years of university study;
- BTEC Higher Apprenticeships (Level 4/5).

9. Degree courses at UK universities

In this section, we give a brief overview of UK HEIs (Higher Education Institutions) that students can apply to via UCAS. There are many reasons for going to university, and students can weigh up the benefits and the costs before making their own choice.

UCAS, the pros and cons of university:

https://www.ucas.com/applying/you-apply/what-and-where-study/study-options/pros-and-cons-university

In order to make a truly informed choice, students should be encouraged to do in-depth research on:

- compulsory and optional modules;
- assessment weighting on exams, coursework, dissertation and so on;
- extracurricular opportunities while at university;
- placement year;
- links with overseas universities;
- university career services and opportunities for mentoring, work experience;
- destinations of graduates/graduate employment.

There are many different types of undergraduate degree courses available:

- bachelor's degrees (BA and BSc, LLB, ChB, MBBS, BEng, MEng etc.);
- Foundation years/Foundation degrees;
- Diploma in Foundation Studies (Art and Design);
- Degree Apprenticeship;
- BTEC Higher National Certificates (HNCs/Level 4), which are equivalent to the first year of university;
- BTEC Higher National Diplomas (HNDs/Level 5), which are equivalent to the first two years of university.

The Blair government's expansion of Higher Education around the turn of the millennium marked a huge expansion of university places. Around 35% of UK 18-year-olds go to university, a number that peaked in 2021 at 38.2%. Despite declining numbers, UCAS has predicted that this number will increase in years to come on their 'Journey to a Million' applicants. University remains a popular route, with around 750,000+ students typically applying to a UK university each year and around 640,000 entering.

Degree courses are mostly three years, but the duration of degree courses can vary from two-year compressed degree courses to four years for Scottish degrees and four years for an integrated master's degree. Sometimes, there is an option to add a year with study abroad or a placement year. Medicine and Veterinary Science typically take longer, up to six years. Undergraduate studies can lead to postgraduate qualifications such as a master's degree (MA/MSc) or a research degree such as a PhD.

Postgraduate study: https://www.ucas.com/postgraduate

The landscape is fast-changing, and students should check if a degree is required for roles they are interested in. For example, apprenticeships offer routes for students who aspire to become lawyers, architects or doctors. For students who aspire to join a particular profession, they should research whether a degree is required for their chosen career and research into the various possible routes.

> **PRACTICAL TOOLS AND TIPS**
>
> Unifrog has a 'special opportunities' section that allows students to research into scholarships, and so on. For example, students in Year 12 (before March) can apply for a scholarship that funds them in Year 13 and guarantees them training to become an officer with the Royal Navy, British Army or Royal Air Force and then serve for a minimum of four years. They can apply for a scholarship or bursary if they are studying university subjects including Science, Technology, Engineering, Maths and Healthcare.

10. Degree courses at US and international universities

We explore US and international university admissions in Chapter 8. Every year around 1,600 students apply from the UK to US universities, and it is estimated that around 500 enrol. Students generally apply via the Common Application; however, there are some US universities outside the Common App, such as Georgetown and MIT. The cost of a US university education is approximately $70,000 per year, making it unaffordable for the vast majority of students. However, bursaries and scholarships are available in limited numbers, though they are often very competitive.

The Fulbright Commission supports academic exchange between the US and the UK at undergraduate and postgraduate levels. They run the annual USA College Day in London: https://www.fulbright.org.uk

The Sutton Trust is dedicated to widening access to university opportunities for state school students in the UK. Students can access test preparation and mentoring via the Sutton Trust. Their US programme involves two residentials in the UK and a week at a US university: https://us.suttontrust.com/how-to-apply

A UK degree with a year abroad in the US can be a good alternative to committing to a US university for the whole duration, though students should consider the fee implications and other expenses.

Increasingly, students also want to explore international university options, especially if they have connections with these countries and an EU passport. Each system has its own application process, and here are some examples of the different deadlines:

- For Canadian universities, the deadline is usually in January. The typical A level requirement is A, A, A (though it can be lower for certain courses), and students apply directly to the university.
- For the Netherlands, students typically need a minimum of B, B, B at A level (though some programmes, such as the University Colleges, will expect higher), and they apply through the 'Studielink' portal, with two deadlines: 15 January for the Early Bird deadline or 1 May for the General deadline.
- German universities require applications through 'Uni-assist'. Entry requirements typically include three A levels with a deadline of 15 July.
- 'Study Options' offers free information, advice and an application service for students, which is funded by universities in Australia and New Zealand. The deadlines vary: https://studyoptions.com/how-apply/

11. Gap Years and post-qualification applications

The Gap Year has a long history that dates back to the 'Grand Tour' of cultural hotspots across Europe. Planned Gap Years also make possible a second university application, giving another chance to secure university offers. Students may also want to mature before they go to university, particularly if they are young in their year group. They may gain relevant work experience or earn money to help while at university. Some international students may be required to do military service in their home country before they go to university. Nowadays, students have various motivations to either:

- apply in Year 13 for a deferred university place (for entry to the following year) or
- achieve their KS5 qualifications and then apply with their results.

Unplanned Gap Years are more difficult. In scenarios where students underperform in exams and miss conditional offers, they may end up pursuing exam re-takes and a new university application. If students can progress to university via Clearing in August, that is often preferable; however, individual choice and personal circumstances should determine the most suitable route.

Gap Years can last 14+ months, from Year 13 exams finishing in May for the International Baccalaureate Diploma Programme and June/July for A levels until enrolment at university, typically in the following September. Students need to plan and organise how they will fill this time. For example, students might want to consider the Year in Industry, a 12-month paid placement. However, students applying for Maths at university are often advised not to take a Gap Year. Students should check university policies on this; for example, the University of Edinburgh does not accept deferred entry for Medicine. Encourage students to weigh up the costs and benefits, opportunities and risks of a Gap Year and look at their plan with them. One suggestion for promoting this option in your school or college is to maintain contact with past Gap Year students and invite them back to share their experiences with current students.

Year in Industry: https://www.etrust.org.uk/programmes-platinum-placements
UCAS Gap Years: https://www.ucas.com/discover/gap-years
Gap Year Association: https://www.gapyearassociation.org

12. Access to Higher Education courses

Further education colleges offer access to Higher Education (access to HE) for students who are 19+ or mature students. They are typically one-year Level 3 courses (equivalent to A levels) suitable for students who have been outside formal education or who don't have the qualifications needed to progress straight to Higher Education.

1| Understanding the Options for Students beyond School or College

13. Setting up a business, enterprise or other entrepreneurial activities

Some young people are entrepreneurs and self-starters who will find their own work and might prefer to pursue their own route outside education, traditional employment or conventional training routes described in this book. You may want to consider how you can support these students in gaining the skills and resilience they need or help them to set their own goals. Whether it be setting up a business, pursuing a dream such as photography or design, or becoming an adventurer or athlete, some students will want to follow their own unique path, beyond the conventional routes that are typical in your setting.

16-19 options

One factor that influences post-18 options is what students have chosen to do post-16. There are many post-16 options, including the following:

- A level;
- International Baccalaureate Diploma Programme (IBDP);
- International Baccalaureate Career-related Programme (IBCP);
- BTEC Nationals (Level 3);
- BTEC Apprenticeships (Level 2 & Level 3);
- Cambridge Technicals (Level 2 & Level 3)
- BTEC Extended Diploma (Level 3);
- T level;
- Apprenticeships.

For 2025, some BTEC courses will be phased out for T levels; the government will 'defund' various BTEC courses that overlap with T levels: https://www.tlevels.gov.uk

BBC article on BTEC and T level: https://www.bbc.co.uk/bitesize/articles/znrqp9q

SUMMARY OF QUALIFICATION LEVELS IN ENGLAND, WALES AND NORTHERN IRELAND

Level	General and academic qualifications	Vocational and occupational qualifications
Entry level	Entry (1, 2 and 3)	Entry-level vocational qualifications
1	GCSE Grades 3–1	Traineeship/NVQ 1
2	GCSE Grades 9–4	BTEC first diploma
		Intermediate apprenticeship/ NVQ 2
3	A levels	T levels
		BTEC diploma
	International Baccalaureate Diploma Programme	BTEC certificate
	International Baccalaureate Career-related Programme	Advanced Apprenticeship/NVQ 3
4		Higher National Certificate (HNC)
		Higher Apprenticeship/NVQ 4
5	Foundation degree (FdA or FdSc)	Higher National Diploma (HND)
		Degree Apprenticeship/NVQ 5
6	Bachelor's degree (BA or BSc)	Degree Apprenticeship/NVQ 6
7	Master's degree (MA or MSc)	Degree Apprenticeship/NVQ 7
8	Doctorate (PhD)	

In the UK, there are multiple levels of qualifications. As the table shows, the most basic is entry level followed, by Level 1 and 2 qualifications, which include GCSEs and various equivalent qualifications such as national vocational qualification (NVQ) and apprenticeships. Level 3 qualifications include A levels, the IB Diploma, T levels and various other equivalents. There are many ways in which students can progress towards Level 6, 7 or 8 qualifications. A well-known route is GCSE, A level, to a degree course. However, there are many alternatives: GCSE, T level, Degree Apprenticeship or NVQ from Level 1 to 7.

1| Understanding the Options for Students beyond School or College

Scenario

A student in Year 13 starts the year planning to go to university and tells you that their ambition is to study Sports Science at Loughborough. They are a suitable candidate, hard-working and capable of putting together a competitive application via UCAS. As the year progresses, they show less interest in finishing their UCAS application, and by the end of the year, they tell you that they are going straight into work because they need to earn money immediately and need to contribute to the family finances at home. You talk to the student, hear their voice and try to understand their reasons. What do you advise?

Suggestions

Encourage them to reflect on whether they can help support the family financially while also pursuing their ambitions. If appropriate, discuss student finance, tuition fees and maintenance loans. Maybe suggest that they finish their UCAS application. Reassure them that a UCAS application does not commit them to going, but it keeps the university option open. Have they considered ways they could fund their university studies, such as bursaries, local charities and paid work during the holidays or part-time work close to the university or at the university itself?

Useful links

- Amazing Apprenticeships, an organisation that promotes the benefits of apprenticeships and tackles misconceptions https://amazingapprenticeships.com
- Careers England https://www.careersengland.org.uk
- Careers Information https://nationalcareers.service.gov.uk
- Choosing a course https://www.ucas.com/undergraduate/what-and-where-study/study-options/how-choose-right-undergraduate-course-you
- Evaluating your Careers programme https://auth.careersandenterprise.co.uk/compassplus
- Government website for searching for apprenticeships https://www.gov.uk/apply-apprenticeship
- Graduate Employment https://www.prospects.ac.uk/
- League Tables, an example https://www.thecompleteuniversityguide.co.uk/league-tables/rankings

- Multiverse, a resource for finding apprenticeships https://www.multiverse.io/en-GB/about
- Post-school options https://notgoingtouni.co.uk
- https://www.allaboutschoolleavers.co.uk/school-leaver-options
- Russell Group https://russellgroup.ac.uk/for-students/school-and-college-in-the-uk/subject-choices-at-school-and-college/
- Squiggly Careers https://www.amazingif.com
- STEM https://neonfutures.org.uk/
- Subject Choice https://www.informedchoices.ac.uk/
- T levels https://www.tlevels.gov.uk
- UCAS information on Apprenticeships, Careers and University: https://www.ucas.com/discover
- University https://www.ucas.com/advisers

> ### Looking ahead: Key takeaways and questions to consider
>
> - ***Staff.*** **A Careers programme should give students exposure to all of the options available to them.** What can you do to help students increase their awareness of the possibilities, reflect on their choices and weigh up the pros and cons? How might you help them make a well-informed decision?
>
> - ***Students.*** **Students are required to have at least one interaction with an employer from Year 8 upwards** to help them think positively about their futures, including apprenticeships and technical qualifications. Consider how effectively this requirement is being fulfilled in your setting.

2 | How to increase students' chances of success

Having outlined various post-18 options in Chapter 1, in this chapter we cover some of the ways that you can help students increase their chances of achieving success. This chapter is relevant both to university and other post-18 options. Co-curricular activities such as clubs, societies and other activities beyond the classroom are a great opportunity for students to develop the transferable and soft skills that employers and universities are interested in. Academic and professional selection processes vary significantly; however, there are various ways that you can prepare students for different applications through work experience, mock interviews, mock assessment centres, super-curricular activities, and (if applicable) preparation for university admissions tests. In this chapter, we cover how students can improve their chances of success with their applications for jobs, apprenticeships or universities. Work experience is important for apprenticeship applications and various vocational university courses such as Medicine, Engineering Architecture and Law. Appropriate super-curricular activities depend on the subject and degree course being applied for; however, reading, podcasts, TED Talks, MOOCs (Massive Open Online Courses) and so on may be suitable preparation for many university applications. We conclude the chapter by covering how you can help students increase their chances of making a competitive application for Degree Apprenticeships and an example of the selection process.

This chapter will cover:

- *practical suggestions on how students can prepare for applications to employers and to universities;*
- *ideas for students' research into careers and work experience;*
- *making a competitive university application: understanding selection processes, admissions tests and interviews;*
- *suggestions for super-curricular activities with some examples;*
- *elements of the selection process for some Degree Apprenticeships.*

Practical suggestions for students

Students typically need a proven academic track record, preferably in the form of public exam results, as well as demonstrating their potential to succeed in their chosen course of study. Schools and colleges can develop courses that help them prepare a competitive application. These courses may include preparation for:

- drafting a CV and cover letter;
- work experience;
- academic qualifications;
- co-curricular activities;
- super-curricular activities;
- university admissions tests;
- UCAS personal statements;
- US university application essays and supplements;
- assessment centres, used by employers to assess candidates;
- interviews used by employers and some universities.

Work experience

Work experience (WEx) is a way to gain skills and insights and is relevant for all students. Some degree courses require work experience, for example, Medicine and Architecture. Students might find out about the workplace and discover it is not suitable for them; this is never a waste of time. Regardless of which post-18 route they are pursuing, encourage students to be proactive and seek opportunities. They can:

- research specific industries, companies that offer work experience, and specific work experience websites like Springpod, Prospects, Student Ladder or The Forage, listed overleaf.
- set up their own LinkedIn profile to connect with employers;
- use any informal connections via family and friends;
- prepare a CV and cover letter to showcase their skills, achievements and interests that they can tailor for particular applications;
- research the company and note the requirements, application process and the deadlines.

WEx can come in various forms: local opportunities, work shadowing or volunteering. For example, they could volunteer for a charity or local community organisation. However, they may need to apply well in advance for a placement. If in-person opportunities are not available, they can try virtual work experiences such as Springpod or The Forage.

Students can further develop their transferable skills through participation in school extracurricular activities such as the Duke of Edinburgh Award. If your school has Unifrog, they can log the opportunity on Unifrog's 'Placements Tool', which links the student, the school and the employer with the relevant forms and requirements. They could also register with the Unifrog tool, 'Talent Pool', which enables them to receive opportunities directly from employers.

Furthermore, the follow up after work experience is important. Encourage students to reflect on what they have learnt, what skills they have demonstrated or developed, and what insights they have gained, so they can articulate this on their CV or personal statement. For example, an applicant for Medicine should reflect on what they have learnt from their observation of medical professionals in their UCAS personal statement. As a courtesy, students should write and thank the people who have made the work experience possible, as this will maintain connections and goodwill.

Scenario

A parent contacts you and requests that you arrange work experience for their daughter, who is very interested in studying Economics at university, and would like you to find a work experience opportunity for her at one of the London banks.

- How will you help students and parents who enquire about work experience?
- What will your work experience policy be?

Suggestions

Motivating students is important, and you can help them see the benefits of work experience. An assembly might be a suitable way to encourage students to organise and try out a range of work experiences, with students in the year above talking about their placements or inviting employers to speak on this theme. Role models are important, so students can aspire, summed up well by the American children's rights activist, Marian Wright Edelman: 'You can't be what you can't see.' Consider how you might communicate with students and raise the profile of different areas of employment or professionals in the workplace.

Rarely, schools might have a member of staff whose role is to coordinate or arrange work experience placements for students. Other schools will encourage students to arrange work experience for themselves. Have an FAQ page for WEx with useful links, send letters to parents with reminders about your policy, encourage students to be proactive and seek opportunities, and organise a careers fair.

National Careers Service:

https://nationalcareers.service.gov.uk/careers-advice/types-of-work-experience

Ideas for students' research into careers and work experience

- **All About Careers.** A career exploration website that helps students with work experience, internships and apprenticeship advice.
  - https://www.allaboutcareers.com/
- **Amazing Apprenticeships.** Explore apprenticeship opportunities across a wide range of industries and sectors.
  - https://amazingapprenticeships.com
- **Bright Network.** Offers internship experiences, including virtual opportunities for students aged 18 and above.
  - https://www.brightnetwork.co.uk/internship-experience-uk/
- **CareerPilot.** Aimed at 13- to 19-year-olds, this site helps students explore career options and find work experience placements.
  - https://www.careerpilot.org.uk/
- **Future Learn.** Offers free courses that provide virtual work experience in collaboration with universities worldwide and various industries.
  - https://www.futurelearn.com/
- **Industrial Cadets.** Programme is an established education charity providing work-related learning and working with students from age seven. It is best known for Year 12 'Headstart' engineering and science programmes and the 'Year in Industry' for school leavers, focusing on engineering, science, IT, e-commerce, business, marketing, finance and logistics.
  - https://www.etrust.org.uk
- **Investin.** Offers work experience opportunities for 15- to 18-year-olds.
  - https://investin.org/collections/our-programmes
- **LinkedIn.** Build your professional identity and network with opportunities for career development.
  - https://linkedin.com/signup
- **Medic Mentor.** Provides free and paid resources for aspiring medical students, including virtual work experience and application support.
  - https://medicmentor.co.uk/
- **Medic Portal.** Offers aspiring medics resources and suggestions for work experience.
  - https://www.themedicportal.com

- **My Big Career.** A charity that partners with schools to support students from disadvantaged backgrounds.
  - https://mybigcareer.org
- **Pathways CTM.** Partners with schools to facilitate students' participation in career events and interactions with employers. It also offers one-to-one mentoring and support for students applying for apprenticeships.
  - https://pathwayctm.com
- **Prospects.** Career information, job search and work experience opportunities for students.
  - https://prospects.ac.uk/jobs-and-work-experience/work-experience-and-internships
- **PwC School Leaver Programmes.** Opportunities for school leavers at PwC, including degree programmes and events to learn more about different career paths.
  - https://www.pwc.co.uk/schools
- **PwC Virtual Work Experience.** Information on PwC's Virtual Insight Programme, offering a glimpse into careers with PwC.
  - https://pwc.co.uk/careers/student-careers/school-careers/our-programmes/insight-weeks.html
- **RateMyPlacement.** Offers reviews of internships and work experience opportunities, along with placement listings.
  - https://www.ratemyplacement.co.uk/
- **Royal College of General Practitioners.** A platform offering virtual work experience for aspiring medics.
  - https://www.rcgp.org.uk/your-career/work-experience
- **Smallpeice Trust.** Offers STEM-related courses and workshops for students interested in engineering and technology.
  - https://smallpeicetrust.org.uk/
- **Speakers for Schools.** Offers virtual work experience and career insight sessions across a wide range of industries.
  - https://www.speakersforschools.org/
- **Springpod.** Provides virtual work experience opportunities and career insights for students
  - https://springpod.com/
- **Student Ladder.** A comprehensive resource for work experience and internship opportunities.
  - https://studentladder.co.uk/
- **Science Work Experience (Student Ladder).** Work experience listings in the science field for Year 12 students.
  - https://studentladder.co.uk/year-12/work-experience-opportunities/science-5/
- **Target Careers.** Offers information about career paths, internships, apprenticeships and work experience opportunities for students.
  - https://targetcareers.co.uk/

- **The Forage.** Offers free online job simulations designed by top employers to help students explore different careers.
    - https://theforage.com/
- **UK Engineering Employers (Target Jobs).** Lists the top graduate employers in the engineering and design sectors.
    - https://targetjobs.co.uk/uk300/engineering-design-and-manufacturing
- **Youth Employment UK.** Offers young people career information, free online courses and work experience opportunities.
    - https://www.youthemployment.org.uk
- **Young Professionals.** Offers apprenticeship and work experience opportunities.
    - https://young-professionals.uk/

Making a competitive university application

There is no substitute for excellent classroom teaching, and no one can avoid the fact that qualifications are required for university entry, whether BTEC, A level, T level or IBDP. From the start of the university application process, students need to be encouraged to meet their academic potential so that they finish Year 13 with the grades that will enable them to progress further. Students should be aware of university selection criteria from the outset.

The selection process

There are multiple elements to a UCAS application, including:

- GCSE or equivalent results;
- Predicted Grades;
- Personal statement (see Chapter 6);
- School reference (see Chapter 7);
- Admissions tests (if applicable);
- Interviews (if applicable);
- Submitted work or a portfolio of work (if applicable);
- Work experience (if applicable, for Medicine or Architecture, etc.).

Admissions tests - Preparation and management

In recent years, the administration of university admissions tests has changed, and staying up to date with the latest test requirements is essential. Many tests now take place externally, and there are many tests required, especially for applicants to Maths and STEM subjects.

Key points:

- UK university admissions tests are no longer administered by schools. Instead, most UK university admissions tests are now taken at independent (Pearson VUE) test centres.
- Students are responsible for registering for these tests by the set deadlines.

> **QUESTIONS TO CONSIDER**
>
> - How will you help prepare students for taking these admissions tests?
> - How and when will you communicate information to students, parents and staff, about registration, preparation and the timeline?

Consider making a resource that collates:

- Admissions tests required by course – for example, Engineering, Computer Science, Law, Maths, Statistics, Economics, Chemical Engineering, Medicine or Veterinary Medicine, and so on;
- Admissions tests required by universities – for example, Imperial, Durham, Warwick, Oxford and Cambridge;
- Admissions tests by deadline – how to register, registration deadlines and test dates.

Examples of admissions tests:

- Engineering and Science Admissions Test (ESAT);
- The Test of Mathematics for University Admission (TMUA).

https://esat-tmua.ac.uk

Key comparison

Most UK universities do not require students to take an admissions test; however, several do (for particular degree courses), including the University of Oxford, University of Cambridge, Imperial College London, Durham University and the University of Warwick. Some subjects require a test, such as the UCAT for Medicine and the LNAT for some Law courses. It is important for students to stay up to date and gather current information from university websites to ensure it is reliable and accurate.

Similarly, US universities have different policies regarding admissions tests. For example, at the time of writing, MIT and Georgetown require students to submit standardised test scores (SAT or ACT), whereas Columbia and NYU remain test-optional.

Interviews and mock university interviews

Students may be invited to an interview for various universities, including but not limited to the University of Oxford, Cambridge and Imperial College London, and for particular courses such as Medicine. Since the lockdown, many university interviews have gone online; however, the 'move back' to in-person interviews is also common. Typically, schools and colleges will need a hybrid approach to practice interviews to support applicants who are either taking their 'real' university interview online or in person.

> **QUESTIONS TO CONSIDER**
>
> - How will you communicate information about interviews and mock interviews to students? Consider having a meeting for all students who may be invited to an interview to share common advice that will benefit them all. Cover the basic information such as what to expect, how to prepare, how to avoid the typical pitfalls, and so on. Maybe include some other perspectives, such as students in the year above to provide feedback on their experience or staff who are interested in supporting mock interviews.

Practice interviews

External companies such as Medic Portal for Medicine will offer practice for Multiple Mini Interviews (MMIs), Panel interviews and traditional medicine interviews. If you are a smaller school or lack expertise, consider teaming up with a larger or more experienced school. You can interview their students, as this gives a more realistic experience of an interview. Incentivising staff to willingly get involved with this, or setting up a partnership, could be considered.

> **Scenario**
>
> It is November. You have a number of students who applied to universities that require an interview online: University of Oxford, University of Cambridge, Imperial College London and so on. These interviews will take place during the day, and the students will be emailed the details about the timings of the interviews. They are unable to take the interview at home for a number of reasons, and you are responsible for finding a quiet office space for these students. How will you respond to their needs?

> **Suggestions**
>
> Find out if other members of the staff can help you. What space is available in the school? Small rooms or office spaces will work. Can you encourage senior leaders to move out of their offices for an hour or so and also provide encouragement? Are there other small rooms that are perhaps used for language conversation classes or even music rooms? Will your school or college be able to provide any technology if needed?

Super-curricular activities

A co-curricular activity might be defined as any activity done outside of lessons, from sports, music and drama to the Duke of Edinburgh Award or membership of clubs, societies or other community activities. These activities are valuable for developing soft skills, such as communication skills or teamwork, and they can develop skills that support certain elements of a university application.

However, in order to demonstrate their interest in undergraduate courses with an academic focus, students should be encouraged to participate in activities that will develop their intellectual interests and skills outside the classroom. A super-curricular activity is any activity that demonstrates a student's interest in or suitability for the course they are applying to, such as reading or listening to podcasts. Background reading is an excellent super-curricular activity for all students. However, each degree course will have relevant super-curricular activities that students should undertake to demonstrate their readiness and help them with their research into their chosen degree course. For example, Law applicants might visit a court of law or sit in on a trial: https://www.thelawyerportal.com. What counts as a suitable super-curricular activity depends on the subject that the student is applying for. Students can engage more personally with their chosen subject through super-curricular activities, which are likely to feature on their UCAS personal statement. In summary, the purpose of super-curricular activities is twofold. First, for students to discover interests beyond the classroom and school curriculum. Second, to demonstrate these interests and their suitability for their degree course, with examples featuring in the personal statement.

There are various companies that offer school and college students research opportunities at a price. If research projects are already available at your school or college, such as an EPQ or an IB Extended Essay, encourage students to pursue these opportunities for research. It will help students take a scholarly approach to a topic and develop their research skills, not only preparing them for undergraduate study but also giving them a specific example to demonstrate their interests and research skills in their personal statement.

Schools and colleges should consider how they prepare students for undergraduate study and what they can do to support them in making strong and competitive university applications. Academic enrichment programmes, workshops and extension work have multiple benefits by helping students develop their academic potential, prepare for undergraduate study and enable them to demonstrate their academic interests beyond the classroom. Academic departments might offer extension classes based on academically challenging material outside the curriculum. These sessions could take place at lunchtimes or after school; however, there are implications for staffing, time and the allocation of school resources, which we explore further in Chapter 4. Alternatively, students could be encouraged to contribute to and lead a session for their peers on a topic that interests them.

ACTIVITY

How will you encourage students to undertake super-curricular activities? Consider suitable super-curricular activities to help students prepare for different degree courses. A list of suggestions for super-curricular activities is given opposite.

Action points to consider

- **Research.** Think about what you could do to support students with their research into universities and courses. Worthwhile research includes the factors mentioned: data such as Discover Uni https://discoveruni.gov.uk, course content, Open Days and so on. They can also attend university taster courses and summer schools.

- **Preparation.** Consider your academic enrichment programmes, extension classes and co-curricular activities and how these activities could support students with their university applications. Examples include reading, podcasts, lectures and so on, with more suggestions below.
- **Interactions.** Consider how you can develop students' encounters with universities.

Suggestions for super-curricular activities

- **University of Bath Outreach Hub.**
  Explore academic and practical opportunities to prepare for the University of Bath.
  - https://www.bath.ac.uk/topics/outreach-resource-hub/
- **BBC – In Our Time.**
  An archive of academic radio discussions on a wide range of topics, including culture, history, philosophy and science.
  - https://www.bbc.co.uk/programmes/articles/2Dw1c7rxs6DmyK0pMRwpMq1/archive
- **University of Cambridge HE+.**
  A wide variety of super-curricular resources created by Cambridge students and academics go beyond the school curriculum.
  - https://myheplus.com/
- **University of Cambridge super-curricular suggestions.** Super-curricular suggestions | Undergraduate Study
  - https://www.undergraduate.study.cam.ac.uk/files/publications/super-curricular_suggestions.pdf
- **Clare College YouTube Channel.**
  Helpful videos about studying at the University of Cambridge and the application process.
  - Clare College YouTube Channel
- **The University of Exeter Free Courses.**
  Free courses on various topics, including ethical fashion, diabetes, climate change and gender inequality.
  - https://www.futurelearn.com/partners/university-of-exeter
- **Future Learn** is a fantastic resource. Produced by the University of East Anglia, it offers 1,400+ free courses to support students with pre-university study. These 'Massive Open Online Courses' (MOOCs) are available for free across various subjects.
  - https://www.futurelearn.com/
- **Gresham College Lectures.**
  A collection of over 2,000 university-style lectures is freely available online.
  - https://www.gresham.ac.uk/

- **Lawyer Portal.** https://www.thelawyerportal.com
- **London Taster Courses.** https://www.london.ac.uk/study/taster-courses-schools
- **MOOCs (Massive Open Online Courses).** https://www.mooc.org/
- **Minds Underground™ Educational Company.**
  Offers essay competitions, online work experiences, debate clubs and virtual summer schools aimed at Sixth Form students.
  - https://www.mindsunderground.com/
- **NYU Summer High School Programmes.**
  Remote immersive courses and workshops from New York University.
  - https://www.nyu.edu/admissions/high-school-programs.html
- **Oxford Digital Resource Hub.**
  Learning resources for students are provided by University of Oxford tutors, including an outreach calendar.
  - https://www.univ.ox.ac.uk/applying-to-univ/staircase12/
- **Oxplore.**
  Encourages students to explore big questions and think critically.
  - https://oxplore.org/
- **Pure Potential.**
  Provides access to events, opportunities and resources to help students explore career and educational pathways.
  - http://purepotential.org/events-opportunities/
- **Turing Scheme.**
  The UK government's international education funding scheme supports students with life-changing opportunities to study or work abroad.
  - https://www.turing-scheme.org.uk/
- **UCL University Study Prep.**
  Free online courses designed to help students prepare for university study, covering essential academic skills.
  - https://www.ucl.ac.uk/study/preparation
- **University of East Anglia – Preparing for University.**
  Short course that explores and develops key skills for success in a university learning environment.
  - http://www.uea.ac.uk/study/info-for/young-people/revision-skills

Supporting students applying for Degree Apprenticeships

Students can consider Level 4 and Level 5 apprenticeships as an 'entry point' with a view to progressing to a Level 6, degree-level qualification. Even though the academic requirements for some Degree Apprenticeships may be relatively low compared with some universities such as Oxford and Cambridge (around A, A, B for A level or 34 points for the IBDP may be required), employers are typically looking for other soft skills and attributes beyond academic grades. For example, many students on a Degree Apprenticeship will have achieved strong academic grades, but they also want students who have developed transferable skills such as teamwork, resilience and communication skills, which we explore in the case study below.

Scenario

A student emails you and asks for help. They tell you that they are among the shortlisted applicants selected for the final interview round from approximately 20,000 applicants to a Degree Apprenticeship scheme. They want you to give feedback on their presentation and help prepare for questions they might be asked in the final round. What do you do?

Suggestions

Encourage them to make sure their slides and content are as strong as possible. Allow them to rehearse and time their presentation to ensure it fulfils the requirements. Check that they have researched the company.

While it is appropriate to help individual students and respond to individual requests, consider how you might also benefit larger groups of students or the whole cohort, such as through workshops or group sessions on relevant themes such as CV or interview preparation or sessions where students can present to one another.

PRACTICAL TOOLS AND TIPS

If you have Unifrog, you could look at the resources for interview questions. Encourage them to think about: Why do they want to work at that company? How might they demonstrate their skills? How would they respond in various scenarios? Reflect on what they have done that makes them a suitable candidate. What have they gained from work experience, part-time work or holiday jobs? Encourage them to rehearse and practise.

CONTEXT AND STATISTICS

The demographic increase in the number of 18-year-olds in the UK over the coming years means that competition is getting fiercer. According to UCAS, there were around 4,700 19-year-olds who began Degree Apprenticeships last year, a small number relative to the population. There are around 170 Degree Apprenticeships available in conjunction with around 90 universities.

Research briefing on Degree Apprenticeships: https://commonslibrary.parliament.uk/research-briefings/cbp-8741

WHAT CAN SCHOOLS DO TO HELP STUDENTS PREPARE, SUPPORT THEIR APPLICATIONS AND MAXIMISE THEIR CHANCES OF SUCCESS?

- Organise group events that will benefit your cohort, such as whole cohort sessions on interview preparation, or organise CV and cover letter writing workshops for a whole year group.
- Share tips on how to go about the application process.
- Encourage students to participate in extracurricular activities and offer the opportunity for practice interviews in the right format, with questions that they'd expect to have in a job interview, not a university interview.
- Stay in touch with former students who have done or are currently doing Degree Apprenticeships and invite them back to meet with or speak to your current students.

PRACTICAL TOOLS AND TIPS

Organise an event (either in person or online) for students and parents that promotes Degree Apprenticeships in various industries and invite speakers from these different industries or students who have pursued Degree Apprenticeships. Attending Apprenticeship Fairs may enable you to make useful contacts. If your school subscribes to Unifrog, you can 'tag' students interested in apprenticeships so you can send them information, updates and advice through the platform.

- Arrange regular meetings for students who are interested in apprenticeships.

- Offer feedback on CVs and cover letters.
- Arrange mock interviews or give students the chance for students to present to a group.
- Consider how you might use UCAS and other resources on Degree Apprenticeships.

QUESTIONS TO CONSIDER

- Consider what you already do to prepare students for when they leave school or college. How can you help each one of your students meet their full potential?
- How will you support students with their applications for Degree Apprenticeships in different areas, from finance or accounting to engineering, retail and so on? How will you track these students and their applications?
- If you are in a school or college context where academic routes and traditional university degrees are typical, how might you limit any 'bias against' more vocational routes such as Degree Apprenticeships?
- If you are in a school setting where few students pursue educational and academic routes, how might you encourage them to consider university?

Case study: Part 2

The selection process for Degree Apprenticeships

Emily Wright, a technology degree apprentice at Morgan Stanley, gives an outline of some of the possible elements in a selection process (Her response to our Q&A can be found in Chapter 1, Part 1 of her case study). We are grateful to her for providing the following text:

It is recommended that students prepare for the various stages below, for example, doing mock interview preparation, practising the skills being tested in assessment centres, researching into the companies they are applying to, and so on.

Online application forms

These could include:

- Grades from GCSE and IB/A level predicted grades;
- Internship/work experience (not necessarily required);
- Languages spoken;
- CV;

- Cover letter;
- Eligibility questions and grades;
- Diversity/equal opportunities form;
- 'Yes and No' questions to check for your eligibility.

Online tests

These could consist of:

- Situational assessment or tests: these questions test what you would do in a given situation. There may be limited preparation you can do for situational tests, but you should be ready to respond to new scenarios.
- A practical tip is to say what you would honestly do; in these scenarios, there's not necessarily a right or wrong answer, but it may be important to be consistent.
- Reasoning tests/deductive reasoning, for example, include some sudokus that you have to complete quickly and accurately.

Assessment centre (online)

This could consist of two interviews, such as:

1. A competency interview based on experience questions. You might be asked to talk through your CV, which gives you an opportunity to elaborate on your co-curricular or extracurricular activities outside the classroom and any other activities, such as volunteering.
2. A commercial interview based on experience questions with a more academic focus. Practical tip: know why you care about sustainability and have done something related to it.
3. A 15-minute interview with an apprentice. Practical tip: be yourself and, if it is a more relaxed interview, you should come with questions to ask.
4. A 30-minute interview with a particular team member, which would be more formal.
5. A group interview. For example, you could be given a logic puzzle. Practical tip: don't try to be the leader, but lead the logic and try to work out as many clues as possible for the benefit of the team.

In-person assessment centres

Individual interviews, group interviews or technical interviews may be used. For example:

- A group interview could involve a logic puzzle where you have to work together as a team because you all have different information. This type of task might test how well you contribute your ideas and collaborate.

- An individual interview with two people or a panel. You may be scored on your responses to each of their questions, possibly without any prompts.
- A technical interview. For example, you could be presented with two or more specific problems, and you are required to use logic to solve them. These could be a test of your logical thinking, and it is possible that you may be prompted to think of different situations.

Insight evenings

These are in person, and typically there may be lots of people in the same room, and you have to talk to them, including senior staff and managers. They could ask you the same types of questions as you get asked in an assessment centre. A top tip is to learn about the company and how it may be a good fit for you. Tell them in advance if you have any issues in loud environments because rooms full of people talking can be very loud.

Video interviews

Be prepared to talk about yourself and the company to which you are applying to.

There could be any number of questions, approximately between five and eight, for example.

Prepare answers to the likely questions, such as those listed below.

A video interview could consist of around five questions with one to two minutes to prepare and two minutes to answer each question. You may have one attempt to record (and can't re-record) your answers. A top tip is to look at the camera, not yourself. Also, if it's a question about your experience, say as much as you can in the time available, and if it's a situation-based question, focus on a shorter, direct answer.

Examples of questions:

1. Why a Degree Apprenticeship?
2. Why are you applying to the specific sector/area of the company?
3. Why do you want to work in this specific role over an alternative role in this company?
4. Why this company?
5. Tell me more about (anything you have written on your CV).
6. What are you most proud of?
7. Tell me about your strengths.
8. Tell me about your weaknesses.
9. Give me your elevator pitch.

Tell me about a time:

10. When you had to work as a team?
11. When you had to work in a team and there was a problem?
12. When you worked in a team that didn't get along?
13. When you had to deal with a person you didn't get along with?
14. When you have had to deal with conflicting priorities?

Looking ahead: Key takeaways and questions to consider

- *Students.* **Successful university, Degree Apprenticeship and job applications require research and preparation.** What can students do to develop their academic profile, super-curricular activities and work experience (as appropriate)? Consider how your students can prepare for different elements of the selection process.

- *Staff.* **Understand the selection process and the different elements of a university or job application.** Consider how your staff can support students, including preparation for admissions tests, submitted work or portfolios and interviews. How can you help them develop the knowledge and skills to make a competitive application? How can students demonstrate evidence of their knowledge and transferable skills?

3 | Understanding perspectives and voices

In this chapter, we set out the different stakeholders in school and college settings who should be considered when managing university applications. Having discussed the range of post-18 options in Chapter 1 and the ways in which students can increase their chances of successful applications in Chapter 2, here we set out relevant issues and questions that are likely to arise between various stakeholders. Our focus in this chapter is mainly on the different perspectives on university applications.

This chapter will cover:

- *a brief discussion of university applications from the perspectives of various groups;*
- *understanding stakeholders: senior leaders, governors and staff;*
- *consideration of the potential misunderstandings that may arise between different stakeholders and suggestions for ways to resolve them;*
- *how to manage a potential misunderstanding between members of staff;*
- *administration vs. inspiration: striking a balance;*
- *understanding stakeholders: students, parents and guardians;*
- *questions for parents to consider and a summary of advice;*
- *the role of 'university destinations' in school marketing.*

> **QUESTIONS TO CONSIDER**
>
> - How might we understand students' post-18 options from different perspectives?
> - What are the similarities and differences between the expectations of the different stakeholders?
> - Who decides which perspective has priority?
> - How might one particular perspective be understood by the other stakeholders?

Understanding stakeholders: Senior leaders

Senior Leadership Teams, including Headteachers and Deputy Heads, have many priorities to balance: academic, pastoral, co-curricular and others. The role of careers and HE advice relates to all of these strands: university applications require academic qualifications, the transition to university is about personal development towards adulthood and the clubs and societies that students take part in (whether sports, music or drama etc.) will help them develop the skills and confidence to make this transition. In short, a school's co-curricular activities will benefit students at university and may strengthen their applications.

Senior leaders are typically very busy people with whole-school responsibilities, including CEIAG. Senior Leadership Teams need to be aware of the opportunities and stakes involved in Higher Education, and you should collaborate with them to find solutions. They should think carefully about how resources will be allocated and the levels of staffing and staff training needed, themes we address further in Chapter 4. Particularly for those in Senior Management who have not held such a responsibility, there is a danger they may not appreciate just how critical the role of Higher Education Adviser is. The staff responsible for managing this process need the time, resources and conditions that reflect the importance of their role. There is a risk that senior leaders might also want to cut costs by appointing a younger or inexperienced member of staff.

Specialist support, time and resources will need to be allocated for any students wanting to apply to universities in the US and other international universities or apprenticeships. In addition, students navigating these choices while on a Gap Year will also need time and support with their applications. School leaders might underestimate the workload involved and the appropriate timetable allocation for staff responsible for university applications.

If a school allows every Year 13 student to apply to multiple universities, including UCAS, the US, Europe and Canada, there will be a cost for staff as well as students involved. Advisers must have the time, knowledge and expertise to advise students; help them navigate the different application systems and process their applications. For example, staff need time to produce accurate transcripts, the expertise to draft and finalise references, manage documents and provide feedback on students' personal statements or US university essays and supplements.

School policies and procedures, as well as resources, will need to be established for the following:

- CEIAG and your provision of career guidance;
- course and university choice;
- predicted grades;

3| Understanding Perspectives and Voices

- letters of recommendation (US);
- UCAS references;
- US Early Decision;
- student's maximum number of US university applications;
- support for students who have missed conditional offers at UK universities;
- staff contact and availability during the school holidays;
- internal school or college deadlines for university applications;
- communication with parents and guardians regarding students who miss internal deadlines.

Senior leaders will need to be aware of:

- the inspection framework that governs CEIAG;
- how far the school or college is compliant and meets the requirements of its inspection framework;
- writing and updating published policies on university admissions and Careers guidance;
- the challenges typically faced by Advisers – for example, students whose parents or guardians only want them to apply to aspirational university choices whose entry standards may be beyond reach;
- reforms and changes in university admissions requirements, such as UK and US university policies on admissions testing;
- the importance of enforcing robust policies around predicted grades and the number of applications allowed, as well as managing the expectations of parents and students on this issue;
- the requirement for a policy on the school website about provider access.

QUESTIONS TO CONSIDER

- Who will draft, finalise and update your school policies on the following: CEIAG, university admissions and pastoral care/personal development?
- How do pastoral care and PSHE relate to CEIAG?

Understanding stakeholders: Governors

Governors are responsible for the strategic management, safe running and financial viability of a school or college. Governors appoint the Headteacher. Governors need the educational institution they are responsible for to be compliant and ready for inspection. Governors should also know how to monitor the quality and delivery of CEIAG. How many students progress straight to university? How many take a Gap Year? How many go straight into employment, apprenticeships or further training? They need data and evidence at various points in the year. For example, the number of offers made in the application cycle (from October), the number and proportion of Year 13 students invited to a university interview (from December), the number who gain a place following an interview (from January), and the percentage of students gaining a place at their 'Firm choice' university (from August), something which we explore further in Chapter 5. This will help them understand the pattern of the year and the different pressure points during the application cycle. Governors are likely to value information about post-18 progression or a university destinations list as an important measure of educational outcomes. Governors also need evidence of the quality of CEIAG delivery and how effectively Gatsby Benchmarks are being met. The Department for Education expects schools to track student engagement with CEIAG. Typically, this is measured by the Compass+ tool provided by the Careers and Enterprise Company.

It is important to remember that governors are also volunteers, and their time is precious and valuable. Your role is to collaborate with them and ensure that they have the information they need to understand your school or college and the needs of your students. It is essential that governors are educated about the Higher Education landscape and appreciate that the school's provision is limited by the resources allocated to it. For example, depending on the size of the Sixth Form, a teacher who is teaching a full timetable (typically the Head of Sixth Form) who is also responsible for the entire UCAS admissions process, as well as taking on other duties within the school, is unlikely to have the time to organise and deliver the specialist support required for applicants to UK, US and other international universities.

It is important that the governor's and staff's priorities align. It is in everyone's best interest that governors understand the processes and work that take place to help students meet their university offers. Without a clear understanding of who is responsible for supporting students and how it is organised, governors cannot ensure that adequate funding or support is budgeted for the staff responsible.

Governors need to consider what support is in place for individual students to explore different options so they can monitor the quality of advice given to all students. Make sure that your report is data-driven and makes clear links between your plan of support and the outcomes achieved.

For example, governors might want to know if your support for students applying for Degree Apprenticeships is as strong as your support for applicants to UK or US universities. Governors should be aware of the legal requirements of schools in relation to CEIAG.

3| Understanding Perspectives and Voices

Governors will need to be aware of:

- the inspection framework that governs careers and Higher Education guidance;
- evidence that your school or college offers outstanding CEIAG;
- patterns and trends over time in university applications from your school or college;
- the factors affecting university admissions and the influences on student choices;
- changes in the US, UK and international university admissions landscape;
- the expertise and time required to develop a team responsible for Higher Education advice and university applications;
- how school policies can inform students and parents and protect staff (for example, policies on predicted grades, the total number of US and international applications permitted by your school or a policy on US Early Decision applications);
- the expectation that schools and colleges might be required to publish how much time is allocated to staff response for CEIAG.

QUESTIONS TO CONSIDER

Assume there are 150 students currently in Year 12 who will be applying to university when they are in Year 13. What timetable allocation should be given to the member of staff responsible for supporting students with these applications? What assistance, and under what employment conditions, should he or she receive from other members of staff? Should there be separate members of staff responsible solely for apprenticeships, and another for US university applications and another for international university applications? What level of resourcing should be in place for the staff supporting students with applications that could be outside of school departments such as Medicine, Engineering, Law and so on?

QUESTIONS TO CONSIDER

- How will your school or college resource support for university applications?
- Consider the value that a Headteacher should place on resourcing Higher Education information and advice.
- Do you have a link governor? Who on your governing body has recent expertise in this fast-changing area?

Understanding stakeholders: Staff

In the past, the priority of teaching staff around delivering a curriculum subject and teaching lessons could have superficially appeared to be 'in conflict' with the priorities of Higher Education and CEIAG. Time and resources spent on students reflecting on their future careers beyond school or college could have seemed like a distraction from day-to-day educational provision and securing top public exam results. After all, the achieved grades are a prerequisite for university entry. Some teachers might have believed that it was enough to teach students well and have been reluctant to deliver CEIAG.

However, the updates to the Gatsby Benchmarks require careers to be embedded in the curriculum. Teachers need to feel that they have the time and expertise to deliver CEIAG, as well as be convinced it is a vital part of their students' education.

After all, excellent classroom teaching is key to successful university applications. Subject teachers can inspire their students' interest in a degree course related to their subject discipline. For example, a Biology or Chemistry teacher might be able to inspire as well as offer practical support for students applying for Medicine, Dentistry and Veterinary Science; a Physics teacher for prospective Engineers; or a Classics or Psychology teacher for Law applicants.

Responsibility for the delivery of your programme should be shared by all teaching staff.

If you are building a CEIAG programme, teachers are your biggest ally and asset, and some of your provisions can be delivered in curriculum time. Consider what your colleagues are already doing to inspire students in their particular subjects. Also, consider the role and responsibility of your pastoral team and Form Tutors.

ACTIVITY

Think of additional ways in which staff in your school/college could support your students with their university applications. Here are some examples:

- Teachers who have recently graduated share their experiences of their course and/or university on a panel, which answers submitted as well as spontaneous questions from a Year 12 or Year 13 audience.
- Heads of Department offer feedback on personal statements and prepare students for mock interviews.
- Staff teaching related subjects support applicants for degree courses.

3| Understanding Perspectives and Voices

Scenario

In order to meet Gatsby Benchmark 5 'Encounters with Employers and Employees', you organise a new careers event known as 'Masterclass' for Year 8. You contact the Head of Year by email to request that the year group has time allocated to this during the school day. You plan to invite alumni and parents to give a series of talks on a range of career areas, with Year 8 students opting to attend different sessions, for example, on Engineering, Medicine and Law. The Head of Year replies, informing you that there isn't time in the students' and teachers' already busy schedules. You discuss this further with them, and they explain that 'we don't want to perpetuate the idea that everything they do now is about getting a job'. They tell you that valuable classroom time should not be given up for Careers Information Advice and Guidance because this year group especially needs to stay focused on their academic work and lessons.

Suggestions

There are two issues for you to consider here:

- First is the timing and logistics of the event. Student attendance at this event is important, but the timing could be flexible. Try to find a compromise by either limiting the time needed for the event or scheduling it for an alternative time in the school day, such as lunch or after school. Alternatively, scale down the plan so that you have a series of voluntary lunchtime talks spread throughout the year.
- The perspective of the member of staff requires understanding. It is essential that you collaborate well with the Head of Year. In the conversation, explain that while you respect their views, you can also gently reiterate that the school is required to offer at least one interaction a year with an employer, from Year 8 upwards. You can respect their view that education is for its own sake, but it doesn't follow that CEIAG is unimportant or unnecessary. You could collaborate with them and agree on a shared plan.

Administration vs. inspiration: Striking a balance

Consider what you are trying to do in your school or college. Be clear about your role and the priorities and responsibilities of the staff who advise students. Is your strength administration? Are you focusing enough on collective and individual advice to students? Have you got the balance right? Have you been given adequate time to be able to fulfil all your responsibilities? Are you also a classroom teacher? Consider how these roles might work together.

- Be clear about your aims and priorities. Are you motivating students? Are you guiding them? Are you helping them to make informed choices? Are you processing applications? Are you coordinating staff?
- Be clear about the extent of your responsibilities and priorities. Will you meet all students individually? Will you meet with their parents? If so, will these parent meetings be planned or available on request? There is an important distinction here between individual and collective parent meetings. It is unlikely that you will have the time to schedule individual appointments with each and every set of parents. However, you can plan some whole-year-group meetings, for example, for all Year 12 parents, when you can cover generic information, practical tips and advice.
- Be clear about your availability. Within what time period can students expect a response from you and the other staff involved? Will you be available during the school holidays or on weekends?

QUESTIONS TO CONSIDER

Various factors influence the different perspectives of stakeholders. What is the 'normative model' for guidance in your context? Reflect on the models for guidance that are influential at your school or college. These may be one or more of:

- a pastoral approach based on students' wellbeing, character, attributes and personal development;
- an academic-focused or subject-specific approach based on intellectual development and academic rigour;
- a co-curricular approach based on developing students' skills, soft skills and participation;
- a career-focused approach based on professional guidance;
- a spiritual approach based on finding a 'vocation'.

Discuss the following questions:

1. Which of these models (or combination of models) is influential in your school or college setting?

> 2. In your school or college context, how do these models (or other similar models) influence the way that 'normal guidance' is understood?
> 3. Consider the stakeholders: governors, senior leaders, staff, parents and students. How might each of these models appeal to or be influenced by the perspectives of the different stakeholders?

Understanding stakeholders: Students

Chief executive of UCAS, Jo Saxton, in August 2024, suggested that students may receive conflicting advice from schools and parents. While parents might want their daughters and sons to pursue a degree course that could secure them a high salary, schools are likely to advise students to pursue a passion or find a course that genuinely interests them. Students can decide on their motivation for pursuing a degree course; they can be aware of their potential earnings and pursue a course that interests them.

Whichever course students choose, they will need to be proactive and build their CV and work experience while at university in order to compete for graduate roles.

You could look at recent data and research into how young people feel about their future and their job prospects. Some are optimistic; others will need encouragement. Still others may need to be reminded that they should have agency and be in control of their lives. They need to make informed choices. They need to be aware of the options, be open to opportunities and plan accordingly (see Chapter 1).

There are multiple factors that might shape students' attitudes towards their future. UCAS has a research project into the perceptions of young people. One factor determining their choice might be their KS5 qualifications and their success – at A level, BTEC, T level, IBDP or IBCP. Another factor is subject choice; UCAS data suggests that too many students pick the wrong KS5 subjects. Indeed, choosing the right subjects for the university course they may want to apply for is essential.

Every school and college has its trends in terms of popular subjects and university courses. However, these trends shouldn't influence a student's individual choice. Following the crowd is not advisable when it comes to university admissions or job applications.

Students might be influenced by rankings, league tables or group membership; however, students should make their own judgement about their relevance. QS University World Rankings is an international university league table, published each year. Others include *The Times Higher Education* World University Rankings, *The Guardian*, the Complete University Guide, and the Academic Ranking of World Universities (ARWU). Furthermore, there are subject-specific rankings, which show that highly ranked courses are not always at high-ranking universities.

Universities can be classified according to group membership. The Russell Group refers to a group of 24 research-intensive universities in the UK, most with a global reputation for their quality of teaching as well as research. There are various other groups: University Alliance (a group of 16 professional and technical universities), Million Plus (an association for modern universities), Guild HE (represents 66 HEIs) and the Cathedrals Group (which includes 14 universities with a shared ethos).

Brand awareness is prevalent in university admissions and job applications. Students are encouraged to think beyond brands and look in detail at the courses on offer or specific companies advertising jobs. Students should also be encouraged to think about how universities market themselves, with photos taken on sunny days. Students should consider practicalities such as how they will travel from one site to another, social activities and sports facilities. The best advice for students is to choose to do something beyond school or college that complements their personal interests, strengths and skills as well as their academic background and qualifications. One of the best reasons for going to university is the course because a student has developed a genuine interest in that particular area of study. A significant number of graduate vacancies are for graduates of any discipline, and many students change direction with postgraduate or higher degrees.

Students need to be ready for the transition to university or work, and there are incremental ways they can become more independent.

- UEA MOOC on the transition to university – a resource for students and teachers

https://www.uea.ac.uk/study/information-for/young-people/preparing-for-university-mooc

Advice for students - Some suggestions
- **Follow your own path.** Pursue what genuinely interests you and find your own direction.
- **Consider influences.** Reflect on the factors shaping your interests and step back to gain perspective.

- **Stay true to yourself.** Avoid being overly influenced by what your friends or the rest of your year group are doing.
- **Communicate with parents or guardians.** Be honest and open with your parents or guardians about what you want to explore next.
- **Be kind to yourself.** Don't be too hard on yourself if things don't go as planned with university or job offers or if your exam grades fall short of expectations. It is fine if you need to go with Plans B and C.
- **Research.** In Chapter 5, we discuss how they can research into different undergraduate courses and the graduate job market.

Things for students to avoid - Some suggestions
- **Over-reliance on the school or college.** Don't expect the school to secure your place at the university of your choice.
- **Overvaluing university brand.** Avoid assuming that the university's brand name will automatically guarantee you a top graduate job.

> **QUESTIONS TO CONSIDER**
>
> - Have students considered all their options, from apprenticeships to Degree Apprenticeships to UK, US or international universities? Entrepreneurship is another option many students will consider.

> **ACTIVITY**
>
> - What factors influence student choices of university/college and course, and possibly employment, in your school/college?
> - List and evaluate these different factors; for example, financial reward, work-life balance, geographical area, family tradition and personal ambition.

Understanding stakeholders: Parents and guardians

Students' post-18 choices, whether to go to university, go straight into the workplace or pursue an apprenticeship, have financial implications for parents and are affected by such matters as choice of accommodation as well as the university itself. For example, living expenses are much higher for a London-based student than for one living in St Andrews, although travel costs, accommodation and other living expenses should also be considered.

Given the costs of a university education and the stakes for each student, gone are the days of making five UCAS choices without careful consideration of these factors, among others. Students are more strategic and global in their outlook and want to consider all their options, from work and Degree Apprenticeships to applying to universities abroad. Increasingly, a global perspective on university entry is the norm for many. Parents will expect schools or colleges to support their daughter or son in making multiple applications to UK, European, Canadian and US universities. Parents may be interested in your school or college's HE programme for the whole cohort as well as the individual support their son or daughter receives.

There is information especially for parents at www.ucas.com/parents, including video guides and a link to sign up for the monthly parent newsletters. For parents looking at US or other international university destinations, The University Guys' website (https://www.theuniversityguys.com/) offers a plethora of information about different university systems worldwide.

Parents should help their children become independent. Progress reports and parents' evenings are the ways that schools communicate. University is not like school or college, and students and parents should not expect 'more of the same'. It is equally important for schools to allow students to become independent learners: the transferable skills they are acquiring at school and what they are learning about how to look after themselves are just as important.

UEA on the transition to university: https://www.uea.ac.uk/study/information-for/parents/faqs

UCAS advice for parents, guardians and carers: https://www.ucas.com/discover/advice-parents-guardians-and-carers

University of Cambridge: advice for Parents and Students Parents, Guardians and Supporters: https://www.undergraduate.study.cam.ac.uk/parents

University of Oxford: advice for Parents and Students: https://www.ox.ac.uk/admissions/undergraduate/increasing-access/ug-digital-resources

This is a summary of advice and the sorts of things you could encourage parents to think about.

Questions for parents to consider

- What academic subjects is your daughter or son good at? What subjects do they have a passion for?
- In what way should and will you be involved in their university applications?

3 | Understanding Perspectives and Voices

- What is an appropriate level of encouragement, interest and support? What are the risks of excessive 'parental help'? To what extent is your knowledge current?
- How can you create the conditions for your daughter or son to feel autonomous and self-motivated about their university application?

Summary of advice to parents

- **Be positive.** Stay optimistic about their future and encourage them to view the next steps as opportunities.
- **Foster independence.** Let them experiment with their decisions and allow them the space to grow by stepping out of their comfort zone.
- **Keep an open dialogue.** Advise and help, but don't impose your preferences. Discuss openly what they want to do next and why.
- **Encourage self-awareness.** Help them recognise their academic and personal strengths.
- **Choosing a suitable course.** Encourage them to pick a degree course they are passionate about, not just one with perceived prestige or employment prospects.
- **Have backup plans.** Balance optimism and realism. Ensure they have a Plan B (and possibly Plan C) alongside their Plan A. If Plan A doesn't work, they can move on to other options.
- **Attend Open Days.** Suggest they attend taster or Open Days during holidays to explore their options.
- **Make realistic choices.** Guide them in making realistic university decisions based on their academic performance and predicted grades.
- **Consider a Gap Year.** Discuss the possibility of a Gap Year and the timing of university applications, including whether to apply after exam results.
- **The personal statement.** Encourage them to draft and revise their personal statement during the summer of Year 12.
- **Stay on track.** Remind them to meet both internal school deadlines and external university application deadlines.

Things for parents to avoid:

- Do not expect the school or college to micromanage every detail of the university application process.
- Steer clear of boasting about their application, offers or achievements to others, as this can raise the stakes for students in a way that isn't helpful for them.
- Don't give them the impression that everything right now depends on the outcome of a university, apprenticeship or job application. Many students take longer to find their way and need to gain experience in order to make a more informed choice.

> **QUESTIONS TO CONSIDER**
>
> - How can your school or college collaborate with parents? Consider how you will communicate with your parents via emails, letters and invitations to Higher Education and Careers events.
> - How might parents be able to support the work of your school or college?
> - To what extent does your parent and student body think of university applications beyond their school's national borders?
> - How far might you educate parents about the current HE landscape, or will you focus exclusively on the students?
> - If you decide to educate and inform parents, how might you develop and nurture university contacts who can assist you with information evenings or similar events?

The role of 'university destinations' in school marketing

Many schools publish leavers' destination lists, listing students' post-school university destinations or alternative plans. This list is formally a 'finish point' for schools and is typically used for marketing purposes. However, a list of student names and their university courses actually represents the start of a young person's journey towards adulthood. More important than gaining a place at university is thriving and enjoying life once there.

In addition to compiling university or destination lists, consider how you should communicate 'university offers' as part of your school marketing. Applicants will know the outcome of their applications in March for the US and May for the UK.

The final place of 'accepted' destination only tells one part of the story. It conceals how many applications were supported by your school or college and how many of these resulted in offers. For example, a student might hold offers at Canadian, US and European universities in addition to their UCAS offers in the UK, and they might also have offers on Degree Apprenticeship programmes.

The offer's picture with an article that explains the nuance could be featured on your school or college website. Universities can offer a wide range of options for students. Offers are conditional in the UK and so may not translate directly into places if the student does not fulfil the conditions of an offer. Keeping records of offers across multiple application systems (e.g. US, UK and international universities) allows you to show the full range of offers.

3| Understanding Perspectives and Voices

Scenario

You receive an email from a senior colleague requesting that you write an item for the school newsletter and website, reporting on the Year 13 university offers. The senior colleague wants the school to publicise and showcase the level of success, focusing on the offers received by the University of Oxford, the University of Cambridge and other Russell Group universities. How do you respond?

Suggestions

There are two issues to consider. First, your response to the colleague's email. If you have time, respond with a brief reply suggesting you meet them to discuss this further. Second, you should discuss and consider the way that your school or college presents information about university offers to an external audience. Here are some key points:

- Brand names are an unreliable and insufficient measure of 'success'. Consider the other excellent universities on your destination list. For example, some excellent and highly competitive universities do not belong to the Russell Group, such as the University of Bath and the University of St Andrews.
- Offers and places are distinct. Unless a post-qualification application is made (i.e. after public exam results and necessitating a Gap Year), offers are conditional, so students may not meet and will not take up all their offers.
- Some students prefer a degree course that includes a Year in Industry or Placement Year, an element that is not offered at the University of Oxford or the University of Cambridge.
- Some of your most capable students may choose not to apply to these universities. For example, the intensity of the eight-week terms and traditional assessment methods at Oxford and Cambridge do not appeal to all students.
- If you also have offers for Degree Apprenticeships or US or international university offers, they should be included in the newsletter.

QUESTIONS TO CONSIDER

- Consider how you collate this information and gain consent from students to share it. Consider how your school or college website will communicate this information.

ACTIVITY

1. Think of different ways that you could use a university destination list. Consider these examples and others appropriate to your school or college setting.
   - Produce an analysis and report for Governors or the Senior Leadership Team.
   - Share with prospective parents and students.
   - Inspire your current students.
2. Identify scenarios in your educational context where a conflict or misunderstanding may arise between different stakeholders. How might these be resolved?

Looking ahead: Key takeaways and questions to consider

- *Senior Leaders.* **The Gatsby Benchmarks require that career guidance is a central part of your whole-school strategic plan.** What role will senior leaders play in ensuring that careers and Higher Education advice is part of your educational strategy? Who will write, update, implement and enforce your CEIAG policies?

- *Staff.* **The Gatsby Benchmarks also recommend that careers be integrated into the curriculum.** How does support for Higher Education and university applications relate to other departments in your school or college? What are the opportunities for collaboration?

- *Students.* **Students need to be proactive and inspired to think positively about their future.** They should apply for a course that genuinely interests them. They also need a plan with alternative options included. How can they be encouraged to take control of the elements that they are responsible for? What is the responsibility of the student to prepare, research and apply?

- *Parents.* **Parents need to keep a positive and honest dialogue with their daughter or son.** In what ways are parents or guardians involved?

4 | How to structure support based on time and staff availability

In this chapter, we outline the different ways you can organise the university admissions side of your CEIAG programme to ensure that the basic elements of applications are covered, no matter how limited your time or resources. We do not specifically address the careers element in this chapter as other, more comprehensive resources are available that describe managing this in great detail. Here instead, we focus on how you can support university applications in a methodical and organised way. If you have students undertaking a mix of university applications and other post-18 options in your setting, you will need to adjust the plans provided here to account for this. We assume in this chapter that your students will primarily be making applications to UK universities through UCAS, though our suggestions also account for the fact that, in some settings, students may also be applying to US or other international universities.

You may find yourself working under various constraints: enough time but insufficient staff expertise, enough staff expertise but insufficient time or not enough of either. Regardless, the key to running a successful university application programme is to ensure you make the most of the resources and time available to you and to plan ahead to ensure the application process is manageable both for students and staff.

This chapter will cover:

- *staffing your support for students;*
- *the allocation of responsibilities, job titles and job descriptions;*
- *suggested structures with three alternatives (Structures A, B and C) for organising your work;*
- *staff training and professional development;*
- *outsourcing expertise and buying in external service providers;*
- *helping students benefit from your time with a suggested four-year programme plan;*

- *staffing: what to do when you are the sole adviser;*
- *you are not alone . . . making connections;*
- *making the most of contact time;*
- *workflow and how to manage busy times in the year.*

Staffing your support for students

In many settings, careers advice, including university applications, is embedded in the curriculum, and all teachers are expected to contribute to CEIAG. In many schools, this can often form part of a Form Tutor's responsibilities. If budgets are tight, the responsibility for UCAS might fall on an already busy member of staff, such as the Head of Sixth Form who then works with other colleagues to ensure that applications are managed appropriately. In other settings, a school might have a Head of Careers or Careers Leader who also manages UCAS.

Some students may apply to universities outside the UK. In schools where this is a new or emerging trend, staff without experience with these applications might be asked to take on this role. While the administration of these applications is arguably something anyone can do regardless of background or previous knowledge, staff dealing with international applications should anticipate undertaking Continuing Professional Development to gain specialist knowledge in this area, as these applications can be complex. It is also very important to note that international applications operate on a different timescale than UK university applications, with deadlines often falling within UK school breaks. You need to think carefully about this and establish whose responsibility it is to manage these applications and answer the queries that students and parents are likely to have outside term time. If that is you, but you are on a teaching contract, how will you be compensated for the time you spend working on this outside your contracted hours?

In line with the Gatsby recommendations, Careers and Higher Education advice should be a whole-school endeavour; all staff need to own aspects of this process (Heads of Sixth Form, Heads of Year, Form Tutors) or make contributions to this (academic subject teachers and Heads of Department) appropriate to their role in your school or college. It is in your best interest to help your colleagues feel ownership of their portion of the Higher Education and Career journeys of your students, as this will lead not only to a better experience for the students but also a more collegiate approach to getting through some of the more onerous administrative elements of the university advising and application process.

How can you develop a collegiate approach to university applications? Here are a few suggestions:

- Organise CPD sessions for new staff each year in which you explain how university applications are managed in your school or college. Ensure that new colleagues understand who to speak to if they have questions about any work they are expected to take on to support these applications.
- Brief the wider staff body on application outcomes during a whole staff meeting. We find that the start of the summer term is a good time for this. This does not have to be a long presentation but should include details of your students' outcomes. This is also an excellent time to thank your colleagues for the help they have given you and the students throughout the application cycle.
- Offer drop-in sessions for colleagues who are tasked with either writing subject comments and recommendations or writing teacher references for students. Make these low-pressure but informative sessions by having sample references available for perusal as well as offering to answer specific questions.

The allocation of responsibilities

There are many ways that schools and colleges can organise their careers and university advising. In some schools, the Head of Sixth Form, an Assistant Headteacher or a Deputy Head has ultimate responsibility for student advising and applications, with the Head of Careers, Careers Leader, Head of Futures or Head of Higher Education working under them. In other settings, the Careers Leader or Head of Futures/Higher Education/Careers (or equivalent) might be a member of the wider Senior Leadership Team and report directly to the Headteacher.

Understanding the management structure of your school and who is expected (and expecting) to do what is essential. You will need to be clear with your leadership about who is responsible for developing the strategy required to run a successful advising programme and who is responsible for implementing this strategy. In some settings this is the same person, but in others, a team of colleagues works together to provide support to students, with each member of the team having distinct roles and responsibilities.

Responsibility for university applications might be delegated or shared and combined between the following people:

- Careers Leader/Head of Careers;
- the Head of Higher Education/Head of Futures;

- the Head of Sixth Form;
- a team of Form Tutors;
- teachers/Advisers in different subject areas;
- administrative staff.

There are many different ways to organise your Higher Education provision; you may find it helpful to look at how other successful schools or colleges similar to your own organise their time and resources. Having the knowledge and time to accurately advise students on university choices can be quite a large undertaking, especially if you work in a setting where 100% of your cohort apply to university rather than taking other post-18 pathways. In this situation, it pays to spread the load and to give individuals ownership over specific areas of university advice rather than expecting one or two people to know and process everything.

Below, we've detailed some ways you could structure a programme of support, though, of course, your plan may look completely different to these. Key to success is understanding what particular jobs need doing and when so that you can ensure that you have adequate staffing to cover everything.

Job titles and job descriptions

If you are the member of staff ultimately responsible for the overall management of both advising on and processing and sending university applications, you will likely still rely on the help of your colleagues to help you manage some aspects of the process. One of the first things to ascertain when you take on a role is your job description and clarifying who is responsible for different aspects of a student's Higher Education or Career journey and outcomes. You also need to know the school policy on students making applications to multiple university systems.

A brief list of the elements of an application of which the school has a direct responsibility for producing or assisting with follows, along with suggestions as to who within the school should or could contribute.

4| How to Structure Support Based on Time and Staff Availability

Required element	Primary contributor(s)	Additional support	Questions to consider
Advising on course choice	HE/Careers team	Academic subject teachers	When and how to guide students on the basics of course choice?
Advising on personal statement/ US application essays	HE/Careers team	Academic subject teachers or the student's Form Tutor	When and how to encourage students to draft and finalise these?
University application forms	HE/Careers team	The student's Form Tutor or relevant Head of Year	Consider internal and external deadlines.
Academic transcripts/ records	HE/Careers team	A school administrator	Who will produce these and when?
Drafting and finalising academic references for universities	Academic subject teachers	HE/Careers team	Who may need to proofread references?

Suggested structures with three alternatives (Structure A, B and C) for organising your work

Structure A

A department composed of teachers who have teaching and other responsibilities in addition to their Higher Education work.

In this example, Higher Education roles are part of the Sixth Form team's responsibilities, and the work required is overseen by the Head of Sixth Form. Here, the Head of Sixth Form and the Assistant Head of Sixth Form are responsible for delivering a programme of advice and ensuring that applications are processed. They rely on support from Form Tutors and other members of the teaching staff with specialist knowledge to ensure that the range of university pathways available is clear. Students may have specific staff contacts they can approach with questions.

Depending on this structure and the requirements of your cohort, it could make sense to combine this with suggested Structure B (overleaf) in order to ensure that students understand the full range of options available to them.

Job title	Job description and suggested responsibilities
Head of Sixth Form	Responsible for the academic and pastoral management of the Sixth Form; manages Higher Education strategy; liaises with universities regarding candidates; creates a programme of advice for the entire cohort; supports and assists the Assistant Head of Sixth Form in processing university applications; provides support during and after Results Day; if no Careers Leader is available, advises students on non-university pathways.
Assistant Head of Sixth Form	Supports the Head of Sixth Form in creating and enacting Higher Education strategy; responsible for ensuring timely and accurate processing and administration of applications including managing gathering references; provides support during and after Results Day; if no Careers Leader is available, advises students on non-university pathways.
Form Tutors	Provide support to students academically and pastorally; support students in writing personal statements for UCAS; provide some reference material for students' references; advise on course choices.
Staff providing specialist advice: Medicine/Dentistry/Veterinary Sciences	Likely a science teacher or other member of staff with experience of Medical, Dentistry or Veterinary courses; provides advice and support for these specific applications; advises on university admissions tests required and manages school-based preparation for these tests and interviews.
Staff providing specialist advice: Oxford and Cambridge and highly competitive courses (Imperial, etc.) that require entrance exams	Likely a member of staff with experience in competitive courses; provides advice and support for these specific applications; advises on university admissions tests required and manages school-based preparation for these tests and interviews.
Staff providing specialist advice: US and international universities	Ideally a member of staff with experience in US or international universities or willing to undertake CPD; provides all US and international university advice; liaises with university representatives regarding applicants and arranges on-site visits; provides support during and after Results Day.

4 | How to Structure Support Based on Time and Staff Availability

Structure B

A department composed of support staff that is more broadly focused on Careers guidance.

Gatsby Benchmark 8 requires that 'every pupil should have opportunities for guidance meetings with a Careers Adviser, who could be internal (a member of school staff) or external, provided they are trained to an appropriate level'; in some settings, students may then decide to apply to university, but for other students, work or apprenticeship pathways may be more attractive. Students applying to university after meeting with a Careers Adviser might then become the responsibility of the Head of Sixth Form or another colleague who is tasked specifically with university advice.

Job title	Job description and suggested responsibilities
Careers Leader	Strategic oversight of Careers provision across all year groups, including university applications; works in conjunction with the Head of Sixth Form and Head of PSHE to provide guidance that meets the Gatsby Benchmarks.
Careers mentors	Non-teaching members of staff who may be working towards a qualification in Careers guidance.
Administrator	Ensures that accurate records are kept of student interactions with Careers mentors or other relevant members of staff; works under the Careers Leader to complete relevant administrative tasks for the department.

Structure C

A team composed of teachers who have teaching and other responsibilities in addition to their Higher Education work. In this example, support staff provide the administrative support that allows the teaching staff to provide students with one-to-one and group support.

In this example, teaching staff take on the advising roles and support staff manage the administrative side of applications. In order to sustain a large volume of university applications, as in the example below, the majority of staff responsible, especially the senior Higher Education Advisers and the Subject Advisers, are teaching staff who may have the time they would spend on duties or extracurricular clubs reallocated to Higher Education work. This is an excellent and cost-effective way to give teachers the time to advise students and support them with their university applications, as well as giving them the opportunity to develop their skills and experience beyond their teaching practice.

An Educator's Guide to University Applications

In this structure, the Director of Higher Education and Careers reports to the Deputy Head Academic and manages the work of the other staff involved but is not necessarily the line manager of each member of it; teaching staff who are primarily assigned to other (academic) departments are line managed by the Heads of those departments.

Job title	Job description and suggested responsibilities
Director of Higher Education and Careers	Manages Higher Education strategy; liaises with universities regarding candidates; creates a programme of advice for the entire cohort; provides support during and after Results Day; if no Careers Leader is available, advises students on non-university pathways.
Assistant Director of Higher Education	Supports the Director of Higher Education in creating and enacting Higher Education strategy; responsible for ensuring timely and accurate processing and administration of applications including managing gathering references; provides support during and after Results Day; if no Careers Leader is available, advises students on non-university pathways.
Form Tutors	Provide support to students academically and pastorally; support students in writing personal statements for UCAS; provide some reference material for students' references; advise on course choices.
Staff providing specialist advice: Medicine/Dentistry/Veterinary Sciences	Likely a science teacher or other member of staff with experience of Medical/Dentistry or Veterinary courses; provides advice and support for these specific applications; advises on entrance exams required and manages school-based preparation for university admissions tests and interviews.
Senior HE Advisers (UK/US/International)	Provide advice and support for all applications, including Oxford and Cambridge and highly competitive courses (Imperial, etc.) that require admissions tests; advise on the tests required and contribute to school-based preparation for these tests and interviews.
Head of US and International University Applications	Strategic oversight of US and International university programmes; responsible for all US and international university applications; manages US Advisers/Counsellors; liaises with university representatives regarding applicants and arranges for on-site visits; travels to universities on counsellor fly-ins and attends conferences; provides support during and after Results Day.

Job title	Job description and suggested responsibilities
Heads of Years 9, 10 and 11	Responsible for ensuring that Gatsby Benchmarks are met for students in these year groups; in this model, university-specific advice only begins in Sixth Form, though engagement with all the Gatsby Benchmarks (including Benchmark 7 prior to KS5) is advisable.
Subject Advisers (UK/ US/International)	Teaching staff with academic or work experience in specific areas who advise students on course choices within one area of study (e.g. Law, the Sciences, the Humanities and Languages).
Administrator	Works under the Director of Higher Education and Careers to complete relevant administrative tasks.

Considerations regarding staff resources and training

- How are you resourced to advise and support students with university applications and other post-18 options? If under-resourced, what can you do to make the most of what you have?
- What level of staffing, expertise and experience do you require to support the students in your context?
- What training is available for existing staff and new staff members?
- If staff time is limited, will you need to buy in some services/outsource to an Independent Educational Consultant or company?
- Are there colleagues in other schools who have successful programmes you can learn from?
- Can you collaborate with staff in other schools to form a working group for sharing expertise and experience?

Staff training and professional development

Staff training and expertise are required for all university advising. However, this does not have to be onerous or expensive (though accredited, fee-paying programmes do exist). One of the best sources of information is from other Advisers, especially those who are experienced and who may be operating within a similar school context as you. Don't be afraid to reach out to colleagues at other schools who have the types of Higher Education outcomes that you are trying to help your students achieve. Many people who do this work are only too happy to share what they know. University events are another excellent source of information. Universities will have details of Advisers' events on their websites, and these events are a good way to discover more about courses and the latest developments and are an opportunity to network. Adviser events run by UK universities are free and may occasionally cover the costs of travel expenses and accommodation.

Some schools and colleges will have trained (Level 6/7) Careers Advisers who can offer impartial advice. Some schools may have specialist teachers who can deliver a bespoke admissions test workshop such as the TSA or UCAT. For many reasons, schools may consider buying in services and resources in order to ensure appropriate provision for their students. For example, if your school has no trained Level 6/7 Careers Adviser, you could contact a company such as 'My Future Choice' (formerly COA), which will deliver Year 11 Careers interviews either in person or online, but only if you are registered with them and using their programmes. Other organisations that work with schools include Morrisby, Bridge-U and Unifrog.

If you have recently taken on a role at school related to CEIAG, you may wish to undertake further training and professional development. Some options to consider are below:

Qualifications in Careers guidance such as:

- **'Certificate in Careers Leadership'** (Level 6) is suitable training either for those who are new to career leadership or are wanting to develop their expertise, leading to registration with the Directory of Registered Career Leaders: https://www.gatsby.org.uk/education/focus-areas/good-career-guidance
  If you work in a state school, you can get a Level 6 certificate from a variety of providers, fully funded by the CEC. There are also a number of providers (not just universities) who will do Level 7 diploma courses (equivalent to SCQF Level 11 in Scotland) online or in hybrid, which takes between 12 and 18 months.
- Taught Postgraduate Certificate in **'Career Education, Information and Guidance in HE'** with the University of Warwick: https://warwick.ac.uk/study/cll/courses/careerstudies/ceighe/ceighecertificate/

Worldwide university advising:

- Times Higher Education Counsellor Resources (including the Counsellor Accreditation Programme): https://www.timeshighereducation.com/counsellor

US university advising specific course:

- UCLA Certificate in College Counseling – almost $6,000 at the time of publication, so out of many Advisers' reach. https://www.uclaextension.edu/education/higher-education-adult-educators/certificate/college-counseling

Annual Conferences:

UCAS (UK university admissions) https://www.ucas.com/ucas/events-conferences
UES (US university admissions) https://www.ueseducation.com/schools

> **ACTIVITY**
>
> Do further research into the various organisations below and consider how you might make effective use of these resources, tools or services in your setting:
>
> - The Careers and Enterprise Company
> - The Career Development Institute
> - The National Careers Service
> - My Future Choice
> - Morrisby
> - UCAS
> - Unifrog

Outsourcing expertise and buying in external service providers

You may wish to use an outside company for many reasons. Students often respond well to hearing the viewpoint of people outside their school or college setting; bringing in outside voices allows you to widen your students' viewpoints by giving them access to expertise beyond your staff body. External providers can be used for widening viewpoints (e.g. presenting to students about opportunities they may not have previously considered) or can provide academic support (e.g. you could arrange for an external company to offer a UCAT preparation workshop for applicants to Medicine). However, you may want to monitor and evaluate the quality of the course you are hosting and ask students for their feedback.

Some external providers charge for their time or their services; this should be clearly stated on their websites and in any correspondence that you have with them. If in doubt, ask. Depending on your school context and the service you would like them to provide, there may be room for negotiation regarding price or the way a service is delivered. Remember, consultants and external service providers are keen to work with your students, and you are the key to allowing them access. Some consultants are happy to make presentations or to run workshops for your students free of charge.

Examples of external service providers

- *Pathway CTM* – offers 15-minute one-to-one meetings on apprenticeships.
- *My Future Choice* – in conjunction with their testing programmes, delivers individual 20-minute meetings for Year 11 students on Sixth Form choices and Careers guidance.

- *Study Options* – official application portal for universities in Australia and New Zealand; offers information sessions on university options in Australia and New Zealand (no charge).
- *Vela Education* – UK-based experts on US university applications; offer information sessions and workshops.
- *The University Guys* – UK-based experts on worldwide university applications; offer information sessions tailored to your students' interests.
- *Sporting Elite* – UK-based experts on US university athletic recruitment; offer information sessions for students and parents.
- *Medic Portal* – offers a day-long UCAT workshop for prospective Medicine applicants.

Consider whether it would also be possible to collaborate and share resources with another school in your area. Examples of effective collaboration might include a joint careers or university fairs. University representatives and employers are often eager to engage with as many students as possible when they make visits and will be glad to hear that you are inviting other schools to any events that you host.

PRACTICAL TOOLS AND TIPS

Unifrog

With their stated aim to become 'the one-stop-shop' for destinations, Unifrog was co-founded in 2013 by husband-and-wife team, Coralie Colmez and Alex Kelly. Unifrog claims to be the biggest platform for post-18 options, used by around 1.6 million students and 3,700 schools. On Unifrog, students can compare all of their options from universities in different countries to non-academic pathways such as vocational training or apprenticeships using Unifrog's 'Know-how library' and 'Careers library'. For example, Unifrog's 'apprenticeships tool' helps students connect with workplaces and local FE providers. Unifrog helps students to research the many routes to university and the workplace, and it's an invaluable tool, which not only helps young people make informed decisions about their future but also makes the task of managing applications so much easier for schools and colleges.

Unifrog is not free. There is a cost for schools and colleges to subscribe, with options to join for one to three years. A one-year subscription is the most expensive. It is 'free' for students whose schools have subscribed. It is 'free' for parents after the school or college has subscribed; they are able to see all the resources but are unable to see their son or daughter's particular profile.

Morrisby

Morrisby is a Careers guidance and destination platform. They offer one-to-one career guidance via an online meeting with a qualified Careers Adviser. Schools can buy in services that include tracking and evidencing student engagement with Careers guidance. Students can also sign up individually.

My Future Choice

Formerly Cambridge Occupational Analysts (COA), My Future Choice offers psychometric testing and an interest profile, with reports matching students to career areas and one-to-one-interviews for students. They support students from Year 7 to Year 13.

Suggested plans and timelines

Does your school or college allow students to apply through multiple application systems? For instance, will you support a student who wants to make applications to: employers for apprenticeships *and* to UK universities via UCAS *and* to US universities via the Common App *and* to US universities with their own application process *and* to international universities? Some students will attempt to make as many applications to as many different programmes as possible in order to 'spread their risk'. If students are not limited by the number or type of applications they can make, you will need to consider the amount of staff time required to enable the student to do so. Furthermore, parents and students will need to know the amount of time this will involve away from their academic studies, how potentially stressful this might be and how it could ultimately jeopardise their exam results.

At a minimum, the school will likely need to supply references and transcripts for all applications a student makes. This takes time. However, there are other elements of the application process, such as one-to-one advising, that should also be resourced and managed; this can be difficult in a school or college setting where a limited amount of staff time has been set aside for student–staff interactions. The scope of your role and the volumes and types of applications you will be expected to deal with are something you should clarify with your school Leadership Team prior to taking on any role. Before accepting any role within Higher Education, check that your job description covers the detail of the job and takes into account the time-related demands that come with it.

Helping students benefit from your time with a suggested four-year support plan

The following plan is intended to meet the basic needs of students and to ensure that they have a basis for making decisions related to whether they will go to university and, if so, which one. There are many ways to augment and build upon this very basic scaffold, which may be very context specific to your school. You may also wish to consult the guidance issued by the Department for Education (Careers Guidance and Access for Education and Training Providers, January 2023), which includes statutory guidance relevant to the maintained sector as well as a suggested timeline for providing Careers support. (https://assets.publishing.service.gov.uk/media/63b69f3fe90e077 246c83323/Careers_guidance_and_access_for_education_and_ training_providers_.pdf)

How to use time effectively to benefit the whole cohort:

- Prioritise your time for whole cohort rather than individual advice, for example, assemblies and group meetings.
- Host a recorded online information event that covers generic information, timelines and FAQs that you can direct parents to at any point in the year.
- Create a FAQ page to direct students and parents to which covers common questions and procedures and policies at your school or college.

4 | How to Structure Support Based on Time and Staff Availability

	Primary focus	Secondary focus	Additional activities
Year 10	Exploring potential future pathways.	Building a strong extracurricular profile.	Hold a careers fair or invite speakers from your school community to share their careers journeys with students either in an assembly or in smaller groups.
Year 11	Ensuring chosen academic pathway allows progress on onto specific university courses or non-university pathways.	Continuing to engage with non-academic activities (such as work experience, super-curricular activities or summer programmes).	Engage an external company such as My Future Choices or Pathway CTM. Consider pathways in relation to mock exam results (if applicable); are students on track to achieve the grades required for their intended course? If you have strong athletes at your school, arrange an information session with Sporting Elite on university athletic recruitment.
Year 12	Identifying potential courses of interest.	Ensuring that any prerequisites for specific pathways can be met.	Invite external consultants such as Study Options, Vela Education or the University Guys to present on international university options.
Year 13	Applying for university.	Ensuring there is at least one backup plan (and preferably two).	Students should attend Offer Holder Days at universities if available.

QUESTIONS TO CONSIDER

If you are limited in terms of time, what must you prioritise? How can you provide students with the support they need if you don't have time to do it yourself?

- University applications, processing and sending these
  - This is non-negotiable and must be completed within a specific timeframe each year; your time should be protected to enable this to happen.
- Feedback on personal statements for UCAS/support with US application essays
  - Can Form Tutors help with this?
  - Could subject teachers help with this?
  - If you do not have the time or expertise to help with, for example, US application essays, consider contacting one of the consultants above and arranging a workshop for your students at the start of Year 12.
- Support with admissions tests and interview practice
  - Could one of your teaching colleagues offer group preparation sessions for students taking the same or similar admissions tests?
  - Who in your school community could help with interviews? Members of the teaching staff? Governors? Parents?
- Tracking the progress and outcome of applications
  - Is there a school administrator who could assist with this? Think about when you may need the data and what it will be used for.
- Administrative tasks such as reminders to staff and students regarding deadlines and application processes
- Responding to individual enquiries from students and parents
  - If appropriate, can Form Tutors answer initial enquiries using information you have provided them?
  - If you are teaching staff, can you set up a @Careers/@HigherEducation/@Futures email address to keep your teaching emails and other emails separate?
  - Consider when these emails are likely to arrive: at the start of an academic year, after an information session/presentation at school, before A level or IB subject choices are due for Year 11 students. Ensure you have set aside time to answer queries at these points in time.

Scenario

You receive an email from a teacher who suggests that a highly able student they teach would be suitable for a US university, and they ask you for more information about scholarships available and the Sutton Trust. How do you respond?

Suggestions

Thank the teacher for their help with supporting students with university and careers advice; one of your biggest assets in building a strong university advice programme is having the support and help of your colleagues within the school. Send them the link to the Sutton Trust and the Fulbright Commission websites and to any other relevant resources and ask if they would be happy to pass them onto the student.

Ensure you add information about accessing opportunities such as the programmes run by the Sutton Trust onto your FAQs or include them in any online or in-person presentations you hold. Creating an FAQ relevant to your setting and keeping it updated is one way to cut down on the time you need to spend answering enquiries that come up year after year.

Note: To be eligible for the Sutton Trust support, a student must attend, and have always attended, a state-funded school or college (non-fee paying) in the UK.

An Educator's Guide to University Applications

> ### PRACTICAL TOOLS AND TIPS
>
> Which situation sounds the most like yours?
>
> I have limited:
>
> - contact time (e.g. one period a fortnight or one period per week);
> - staffing;
> - staff knowledge – opportunities to Continue Professional Development;
> - financial resources;
> - everything!
>
> Here are some practical ideas about how you could work around these constraints:
>
> | Constraint | Potential solution | Consider |
> |---|---|---|
> | Limited contact time | Provide information to students mainly in group meetings. | Trying to find more time - are there duties you could be taken off of to give you more time to administer the Higher Education or Careers programme? |
> | Limited staffing | Ask your SLT to reallocate the time colleagues spend on extracurricular or other duties to HE work. | Trying to find more time - are there duties other staff could be released from to give them time? |
> | Limited staff knowledge | Provide colleagues with opportunities for development either in whole-school INSET sessions (run by you or an external) or through attendance at relevant conferences or external training events. | Offering drop-in sessions for other members of staff with responsibility for various aspects of the process (references, supporting students writing personal statements or application essays). |
> | Limited financial resources | Many consultants will offer free information sessions for your students (see list above). If you are working in a state school or FE college, the Sutton Trust may be able to provide you with support. | Reaching out to university admissions representatives; in the UK, the emphasis on widening participation means that university resources have often been set aside to support local schools and colleges. US university representatives travel in the UK and abroad regularly and are often happy to visit if they are in the area. |

4 | How to Structure Support Based on Time and Staff Availability

Constraint	Potential solution	Consider
Limited everything!	Start slowly; strong programmes develop over time. Prioritise helping students send strong applications to their target institutions. If you are working in the maintained sector, make sure that you are accessing all the resources available to you through universities or other organisations such as the Sutton Trust.	Speaking with your Leadership Team about the 5-10 year plan for Careers/Higher Education/Futures guidance for students at your school. If staffing levels are not appropriate when you take on the role, there should ideally be an acknowledgement of this and a plan to address it.

Scenario

You have been asked by your Senior Leadership Team to identify students in Year 12 who are underperforming and who might benefit from additional support and an extra meeting to discuss their options.

Suggestions

- When would your Leadership Team like this to be completed? Is it time-sensitive, or can it wait?
- Is there an administrator who can provide you with the data you need? Are there specific indicators of underperformance that your Leadership Team would prefer you to focus on?
- If this request comes at a difficult time of year for you in terms of processing Year 13 applications, are there other colleagues who can assist you?
- Would this group of students be best served by having one-to-one or group meetings?
- Are there other colleagues who need to be involved for pastoral or academic reasons?

Staffing: What to do when you are the sole adviser

Administration and organisation: ensure that you have systems set up to process UCAS applications in good time, with appropriate internal deadlines for students and staff, to ensure that you meet the mid-October and January deadlines. If your students also apply to US universities, note that the Early Application deadlines generally fall just after the mid-October UCAS deadline (generally around 1 November) and just before the January UCAS deadline (generally around 1–5 January). These will be stress points administratively for you.

In some settings, one person, for example, the Head of Sixth Form with no time allowance or limited resources, might be responsible for UCAS applications. A platform such as Unifrog would make it easier to track applications and offer feedback on personal statements (see Chapter 6). External Careers Advisers familiar with Unifrog can be engaged to encourage students to use the sections most relevant for them and to explore their options.

Make time to speak to your Leadership Team about what can be provided to students if you have very limited time or resources. This is where you may wish to contact other schools to ascertain how they manage working with, for example, large cohorts with limited time.

Consider enlisting the help of parents or alumni of your school. Could you ask a group of parents or former pupils to come in to speak about specific careers or university pathways they have taken? This does not need to take the form of a full careers fair but could take place at lunch in a classroom. Could a parent or set of parents with relevant expertise come in and conduct mock university interviews? Would any of your former pupils be happy to act as mentors? Is there a governor who might be able to share their expertise or experience with your students? You may be surprised by the willingness of people to help your school community.

You are not alone . . . making connections

Actively seek to make connections with other people who are doing the same work as you are. Some of these networks are formal, but many are simply loose networks of people who gather either in person at certain times of the year (e.g. at the annual UCAS Conference) or who share information online (LinkedIn, specialised Facebook groups), which we cover in more detail in Chapters 5 and 8.

Networking can be daunting, but if you are able to build a network of other Advisers in similar positions, you can ensure that you have not only professional and personal support from colleagues in other schools but you can also use these Advisers as sounding boards for building your own programme. Remember that at a conference or adviser training day, everyone is there for a common purpose, and it is much easier to make connections with people after a brilliant talk than by ringing someone at another school out of the blue asking for help.

In many US and international schools, colleagues do not wear as many hats as they may do in a British school. 'College counselling' is professionalised and seen as a separate career path to teaching. If you are in a British or international school setting, you may benefit from reaching out to colleagues working in different types of schools than yours, either in your geographical area (or further afield), as their programmes are likely to be viewed and implemented in a different and perhaps more 'ringfenced' way than yours. Most colleagues are happy to help others in similar positions; it never hurts to ask for a short conversation with your counterpart at another school. Knowing you are not alone in trying to manage (what can be) an unwieldy process can be enormously helpful.

Making the most of contact time

Whole cohort vs. one-to-one meetings

We recommend that you employ a mixture of whole cohort meetings and one-to-one meetings, as appropriate to your time and the availability of students.

Whole cohort meetings can be best used to share information that everyone needs to hear and that they would benefit from hearing together (and hopefully then supporting each other through any difficulties that they find they all have in common, such as researching universities). Whole cohort meetings are also useful for other colleagues who may have a tangential relationship with your advising programme to attend; this ensures that you and other colleagues are on the same page in terms of the advice and support you are giving to each cohort.

One-to-one meetings tend to fall into two categories: standard planned meetings that provide students with personalised advice and non-standard meetings that often involve parents or guardians and can occur at any time. Requests for meetings by parents are often reactive; they may be responding to a situation that encompasses more than just careers or university advice. Always consider who else in your setting may need to be involved when meeting with a parent or guardian, even if it is nominally about the student's destination post-school or college.

Workflow and how to manage busy times in the year

Make sure you have considered which groups must take priority at different times of the year and plan accordingly. Students are often happy to wait for advice and support if they know that it will be forthcoming at some point in the year.

Typically, there is work involved in the holidays that makes your work a 'year-round' task. With the exception of 'Advising on course choice', the other elements of the application process happen late in Year 12 or during Year 13. In terms of the focus of this book – university pathways – some elements of the process are fairly static, which makes planning the distribution of the work well in advance easier.

For example, universities will always have application forms that students need to fill out; the majority of worldwide university systems require documentation to help them understand if a student has the academic qualifications to succeed at their tertiary institution (generally a transcript or other record of grades achieved); most universities require a reference from the school in which the school effectively vouches for the student and provides further details as to their suitability for university.

4| How to Structure Support Based on Time and Staff Availability

Time of year	Pinch-point	Solution	Note
Summer holidays between Year 12 and Year 13	Oxford, Cambridge, Imperial, Durham and Warwick admissions test registration.	Ensure that all Year 12 students are informed of the existence of admissions tests and how to register for these.	Students must register themselves for these tests; ensure parents are informed in writing well in advance of the end of summer term.
Start of autumn term	Year 12 and Year 13 students both need advice and support.	Prioritise Year 13 students; they are making their applications first. Communicate the timeline of support to Year 12 students and their parents and guardians. This can help alleviate worry and unnecessary contact from students and parents. Consider how you might respond to the Year 12 students and their parents who may wish to discuss changes to subjects chosen.	Consider holding an online or in-person meeting for all parents and guardians of Year 12 students to explain the support the Year 12 students will receive once the Year 13 applications have been processed (mid-January).
Middle of autumn term	Students making Early Action or Early Decision US university applications generally have an early November deadline, which falls near or just after half-term.	Communicate clearly to any US applicants and their parents early (at least once in the summer term of Year 12 and once at the beginning of the autumn term of Year 13) what support, if any, is offered during half-term holidays.	If you have given parents and students enough notice of when support is available, you should not feel obliged to be on call during school holidays.

79

Time of year	Pinch-point	Solution	Note
December	Oxford and Cambridge and Medicine/Dentistry/Veterinary science interview requests.	Ensure that any student applying to these courses has attended group sessions detailing how to approach interviews.	
End of autumn term and over the December holiday break	The majority of Regular US university applications are due between 1 and 5 January; students should ideally complete the majority of work on these applications during the autumn term.	Communicate clearly to any US applicants and their parents early (at least once in the summer term of Year 12 and once at the beginning of the autumn term of Year 13) what support, if any, is offered during half-term holidays.	If you have given parents and students enough notice of when support is available, you should not feel obliged to be on call during school holidays. Last-minute applications are rarely successful.
Start of spring term	January UCAS deadline – remaining UCAS applications to finalise and send.	Try and spread the work out; remind students that there is nothing to stop them from applying well before the deadline if they are ready to. Enlist the support of the Sixth Form team and Form Tutors to help students who are struggling. Can you run work/help sessions for students who need your in-person support to complete their applications?	Make sure parents and students are well appraised of all deadlines. Remember that while the UCAS 'equal consideration' date falls in January, applications may still be accepted after this date, at the discretion of the university. Students sometimes choose not to meet the January deadline even when they have been made aware of it. You cannot assume they will act on information received.
Summer holidays between Year 12 and Year 13	Post-results support and Clearing.	Students need support during these periods; who is best placed to provide this?	

4| How to Structure Support Based on Time and Staff Availability

Your obligations during holiday periods should be set out in your job description and discussed with your line manager. In some settings, a member of the Higher Education team is employed on a support staff year-round contract; in others, teaching staff are expected to work during the holidays as required by the role. Establish with your leadership what is expected of you, ideally before accepting the role.

Some suggestions to manage workload

- Organise meetings for entire cohorts to address their FAQs and timeline and explain the support available for them. For example, you could plan for an introductory assembly for Year 12 early in September to cover FAQs introducing the support they will receive for careers and university applications during the Sixth Form and reassuring the cohort that you will prioritise them from January (once the Year 13s have finished their university applications). You may also wish to plan for a Year 11 information evening in November when you might have time to address their FAQs and explain your CEIAG timeline.
- Keep a file of generic emails with advice and key points that can be used for students or parents who seek advice outside the times when you are able to prioritise their year group.
- Form Tutors can also be very useful in managing student and parent queries; make sure you provide the relevant information to Form Tutors to distribute on your behalf if appropriate to your setting. Do not assume that the Form Tutors can, or should, field Higher Education or careers queries on their own.
- Discuss with your line manager how you will deal with individual enquiries from students and parents during busy points in the application cycle, including the holidays. Would it be acceptable to use an out-of-office reply to external emails that details what is happening in the admissions cycle and when you will be able to respond to non-urgent enquiries? Being able to direct non-urgent emails to a FAQ is one way to lessen email traffic, which can take up a considerable amount of time to manage.

Looking ahead: Key takeaways and questions to consider

- *Staff.* Supporting students in understanding and accessing the full range of post-18 options, whether that is university, apprenticeships or another pathway, requires time, careful planning and considered use of available resources. What structure do you currently have? How might you make use of time and resources to make this possible in your educational setting?

- *Staff.* **Responsibility for delivering information and advice about universities requires expertise.** What experience and training do staff need to fulfil the role? What time and resources are needed? What role will they play in your school operation and strategy, and in relation to your Headteacher, Principal or Senior Management Team?

- *Senior Leaders.* **Make sure your senior leaders are aware of the work you are doing.** How can they help meet the varied needs of your students? How can they help you develop and maintain links with employers, training providers, universities and relevant members of your school and wider community?

5 | Managing university applications: UK focus

In 2024, UCAS' chief executive, Jo Saxton, identified the potential conflict between the perspectives of schools and parents. She pointed out that when choosing a university degree course, schools might advise students to follow their interests and passions, whereas parents are more likely to encourage their daughters and sons to choose on the basis of their potential future earnings.

There are many motivations for students to pursue Higher Education, but students need to embark on their undergraduate studies 'with their eyes open' given the costs involved, the high dropout rates and the limited number of graduate roles available. In this competitive and fast-changing admissions landscape, we discuss ways you can set up a programme to support students making a UCAS application. We cover the basics of managing a cohort of UCAS applicants, advising students on course choice and how to navigate choices such as Firm and Insurance options. We also discuss how to manage exam Results Day and provide advice for students who narrowly miss offer conditions. We discuss the process of applying through UCAS and where the responsibility for a UCAS application starts and finishes.

We outline UCAS resources and offer practical tips and timelines to manage mid-October deadline applications. We conclude the chapter with a brief look at student finance and graduate employment.

This chapter will cover:

- how to get started: the essentials of providing support for UK applications;
- advising students on their degree course choice;
- supporting applicants to UK universities;
- UCAS resources for Advisers;
- the basics of UCAS for Advisers;
- internal school/college deadlines and external UCAS deadlines;
- supporting UK university applications;
- from longlist to shortlist: choosing five UK universities;
- replying to UCAS offers, exam results and Clearing;

- *advising students about Firm and Insurance choices;*
- *supporting students who miss their conditional conditions;*
- *managing an exam Results Day service for students;*
- *expectations, student finance, costs and graduate employment.*

How to get started: The essentials of providing support for UK applications

The school or college is responsible for the administration of the UCAS application; informing the students about how to start an application, the timeline, the deadlines and eventually sending applications for Year 13 students from September to January. The school is responsible for the advice given to students to encourage them to choose a suitable course and prepare to make a competitive application.

There are over 380 universities, colleges and HEIs in the UK and more than 50,000 courses to choose from, which presents a potentially overwhelming number of options. There will be degree courses they are unlikely to have heard of: Brewing and Distilling (Heriot Watt University), Ethical Hacking (Abertay University) or Surf Science (Cornwall College). There will be degree courses with the same name (such as English or History) that vary hugely in terms of the course content or delivery.

Choices and uncertainty are typically difficult to navigate, but there are various ways you can help students. The best advice is to choose the course first. UCAS Hub is an excellent place to start research. It is free for everyone, and after a student has registered via their email and chosen a password, they have access to multiple tools, 'subject guides' and an 'ultimate guide' to course choice. Your task is to help students research into UCAS courses so they feel reassured and well informed. Pointing them towards these starting points for their research is a good way to begin.

Advising students on their degree course choice

Like buying a car without test driving it, we wouldn't expect students to commit to a course without attending an Open Day or a university taster course. Getting the course right is essential to a student's success: if they are interested in their course and it holds their interest, they are less likely to drop out. In terms of what students should look for in a course, they might also pay close attention to how a course is taught, how it is examined and consider whether it plays to their preferred learning styles, personality type and strengths. They could also consider an additional year, for example, degree courses with a placement year or study abroad. They should understand the different types of courses available:

- **single honours degrees** in the arts and humanities, such as History or English, or in the sciences, such as Chemistry or Physics
- **joint honours degrees** such as History and Politics, or Philosophy and Computer Science, or Data Science and a Modern Language
- **combined honours degrees** such as Arts and Sciences, also known as the BASc at UCL and so on, or Flexible Combined Honours, or Liberal Arts allow even greater breadth

Universities with known specialisms increasingly offer a broader range of courses. For example, The London School of Economics and Political Science (LSE), renowned for Economics and Politics, also offers a BSc degree course in Language, Culture and Society. Similarly, Imperial College London, best known for its STEM specialism, allows increasing breadth, for example, their BSc degree in Economics, Finance and Data Science.

How to choose an undergraduate course:

https://www.ucas.com/applying/you-apply/what-and-where-study/choosing-course
https://ultimateguides.ucas.com/pickingyourdegree/

[Note that there are many other types of courses students can apply to via UCAS – see Chapter 1.]

Action points to consider

Consider how you might also encourage students to attend university Open Days and taster courses. Gatsby Benchmark 7 recommends that students applying to university should attend at least two Open Days. As a result, you might want to arrange a visit for all students or target those who you feel will not have family support to do this, for example, Pupil Premium students and those who are the first generation in their family to go to university. The problem with taking a whole year group is that it is not only a logistical challenge but it might also lead to an excessive number of students applying to one institution based solely on that experience.

Taster courses: https://www.london.ac.uk/study/taster-courses-schools
Calendar of university Open Days: https://www.opendays.com

Liberal arts in the UK

For students who want breadth across the arts *and* sciences, the UCL Arts and Sciences degree awards a Bachelor of Arts and Sciences (BASc). In the arts and humanities, Flexible Combined Honours (FCH), by contrast, often has few or no core modules and allows students to combine two, three or four subjects together. For example Combined Honours Social Sciences at Durham University or FCH at the University of Exeter, for example. In the sciences, Natural Sciences courses offer breadth, for example, the University of Cambridge, Durham University and so on. Alternatively, they could study Politics, History, Literature and Culture as part of an American Studies degree programme, including a year at a US university.

The London Interdisciplinary School (LIS) breaks away from the traditional curriculum models, and disciplinary boundaries, connecting subjects in new ways. Interdisciplinarity (ID) is an innovative approach that develops students' expertise and connections across subjects, focusing on finding solutions to problems and equipping them with skills for the modern workplace. This would suit students who are interested in real-world problems, methods and solutions.

Furthermore, the University of Edinburgh offers an undergraduate degree in Interdisciplinary Futures and the University of Bristol offers degree courses 'with Innovation', which focus on the application of solutions to real-world problems. For example, an alternative to single honours Geography is Geography with Innovation, or instead of single honours Physics, they could opt for Physics with Innovation.

University of Bristol courses 'with Innovation':

https://www.bristol.ac.uk/study/undergraduate/2025/innovation/

For students who are willing to look further afield (explored further in Chapter 8) several Australian universities also offer courses centred on innovation, such as:

Curtin University's Bachelor of Innovation: https://www.curtin.edu.au/study/offering/course-ug-bachelor-of-innovation--b-innov/.

Clarkson University in New York offers a BSc in innovation and entrepreneurship: https://www.clarkson.edu/academics/majors-minors/innovation-entrepreneurship

Arizona State University offers a BA in Innovation in Society: https://sfis.asu.edu/degree-programs/undergrad/ba/

Factors for students to consider

All students should reflect on which factors are relevant to them. Some students will have personal factors that will inform their choices, such as distance from home, travel costs, accommodation or the opportunities to work while studying. For some, an Olympic-sized swimming pool or a strong athletics provision with a running track may be essential.

According to Nick Hilman's 2024 'Higher Education Policy Institute' report, the three most likely reasons for a student to drop out of a UK university: 'mental or emotional health' (29%), 'financial difficulties' (8%) and 'the content of the course is not what I expected' (6%). To avoid this situation, students are well advised to do thorough research, especially into course content and assessment, so they are making an informed decision about their degree course.

Students could also take into account data for their chosen course. UK universities are required to publish data about their undergraduate courses, and it is known as KIS (Key Information Set) data, which includes various elements from teaching and learning to student satisfaction, to graduate employment and so on.

> **ACTIVITY**
>
> How will you encourage students to research into their degree courses? Make a resource that will help your Year 12 students to research into degree courses that interest them, and find out more about the compulsory and optional modules and the methods of assessment. The resource could also encourage them to consider other factors that they consider relevant, such as student satisfaction, graduate employment, average starting salaries levels of student satisfaction, and other relevant factors and so on.

The NSS (National Student Survey) is an annual survey that seeks the feedback of students at the end of their course: https://www.thestudentsurvey.com. The data gained from this survey can be found easily at https://discoveruni.gov.uk. Students might also be interested in the quality of research and teaching for their chosen course, and they can research into this. The Research Excellence Framework

(REF) was introduced in 2014 as a measure of the quality of research in Higher Education Institutions (HEIs) in the UK: https://www.ref.ac.uk. It also took place in 2021, and the next is planned for 2029. Since 2017, the Teaching Excellence Framework (TEF) measures the quality of university teaching, awarding institutions by category: Gold, Silver and Bronze.

https://www.ucas.com/advisers/help-and-training/guides-resources-and-training/tools-and-resources-help-you/guide-teaching-excellence-framework-tef

https://www.timeshighereducation.com/student/news/tef-2023-results

Supporting applicants to UK universities

For UK university admissions, course choice is essential. Students should apply to the course they are best suited to and which will hold their interest for the duration of the degree course. Students should choose their course first and their five universities second; research into course content is necessary.

Students can apply for up to five courses via UCAS. However, there are a few UK universities (at the time of writing, examples include Oxford Brookes, London Northeastern, TEDI, the University of Buckingham, London Interdisciplinary School etc.) and other specialist colleges (for the performing arts, music schools, art colleges etc.) that accept direct applications. This is most likely to be 'a positive' for students, as this allows them an extra option outside of UCAS, or a so-called 'sixth choice'.

Whether it is supporting a student with an application for Liberal Arts at the University of Warwick, Medicine at Imperial College London or Classics at the University of St Andrews, the staff responsible for UCAS applications in your setting will need some expertise.

Firstly, a basic working knowledge of the variety of these types of courses; an understanding of what a Liberal Arts degree in the UK might look like, the unique selection process for Medicine including a personal statement that reflects volunteering, work experience and an awareness of the NHS, and the super-curricular activities that might demonstrate a candidate's suitability for Classics.

Secondly, an awareness of these universities as institutions in terms of their geography, size, foundation and history; the University of Warwick, a campus based near Coventry, renowned for its cross-faculty projects, founded in the 1960s and home to over 28,000 students; Imperial College, the large STEM specialist for over 23,000 students in an expensive part of West London, which can trace its roots to the early 1900s; or the University of St Andrews, a highly ranked and highly competitive but small institution of just over 8,000 undergraduates with typically 10,000 applicants for 500 (Rest of UK, or RUK) places each year. One fun but trivial fact about St Andrews is that it has no McDonalds and no Waitrose; however, more importantly it has a very rich history, having been founded in the early 15th century, and today a Scottish degree course will typically take four years.

Your colleagues' knowledge of specific courses and institutions develops over time and increases with experience. If you are invited to visit a university on an Adviser's Conference or Open Day, do try to attend or ask a colleague. Some universities host annual visits for Advisers; these are an excellent way to understand more about what makes a particular university and their courses are distinctive. It is important that staff can point students in the right direction. Virtual tours, Open Days and taster courses are all excellent ways for students to extend their knowledge and research beyond their UCAS Hub.

UCAS resources for Advisers

While staff will inevitably have different levels of knowledge and understanding of different courses and institutions in the UK, it is a priority to develop knowledge of the process and the timeline. There are excellent UCAS resources and toolkits that offer comprehensive information for Advisers about every element of a UCAS application, with PDF 'Adviser Guides' updated for every year:

https://www.ucas.com/advisers/toolkits
https://www.ucas.com/advisers/help-and-training/toolkits/2025-cycle
 -toolkit
- Each year, an Adviser Guide is produced for staff at schools, colleges and other centres, such as careers offices and agencies, who advise potential undergraduate applicants to HE courses in the UK.
- https://www.ucas.com/advisers/help-and-training/toolkits/adviser-toolkit-supporting-students-individual-needs

If you are tempted to make PowerPoint presentations for a staff meeting, parent's evening or assembly, look no further than UCAS Toolkits, which offer excellent off-the-shelf resources for Advisers: https://www.ucas.com/advisers/toolkits. It is easy to personalise and tailor these to your event if you are confident that you won't lose your audience in PowerPoint slides. More experienced staff might prefer alternative ways to deliver information and advice to various audiences. Depending on the purpose of your presentation, consider how you can hold your audience's interest. Engage them as you would a class; show personality and interest in your topics. You could include anecdotes, quotes or insight into trends at your school or dispel popular myths.

- Student assemblies work well if the information is directed to them at their stage in the application process, with specific instructions and practical tips and maybe a few anecdotes, finishing on an upbeat and positive note.
- Parents' evening presentations can work well if you cover a few key points and invite a range of external speakers, either representatives from a university recruitment or alumni or an employer to speak on different themes.
- Presentations at staff meetings work well if they are short and to the point and relevant for all staff. Staff are more likely to engage if you are brief and encouraging and grateful for their work. They may find it refreshing to hear your voice, with no need for PowerPoint slides. However, other staff might appreciate a copy of the slides, much as students sometimes do. Either way, a summary of the points you made might be useful if staff are absent or missed your talk. Furthermore, a written record or summary will make it easier for you to update in the future if you are likely to give similar talks or regular updates.

> **PRACTICAL TOOLS AND TIPS**
>
> Here are two examples of typical UCAS deadlines:
>
> - Mid-October for early applications to the University of Oxford, University of Cambridge, and for Medicine, Veterinary Science and Dentistry;
> - Mid-January, the 'equal consideration' deadline for all other UCAS applications.
>
> These dates have not changed much for many years, but they could change in the future.

UCAS Apply, adviser track and reports

UCAS Apply is free for registered centres. There is a cost for reports and different levels of subscription: bronze, silver and gold packages. It is not available to parents and students.

https://www.ucas.com/advisers/help-and-training/guides-resources-and-training/ucas-registered-centres/becoming-ucas-centre

The Annual UCAS Conference for Teachers and Advisers

This is an excellent way to meet people who have the same or similar job title to you. Usually, this conference takes place around February or March, and the venue, timing and costs vary. In previous years, the conference has taken place in various cities including Manchester, Harrogate and Birmingham and the more expensive packages have included a gala dinner with memorable speakers (Sugata Mitra, the educational theorist, and Dr Maggie Aderin-Pocock, the British space scientist, have been particular highlights) and the fiercely competitive quiz evenings, in which 400+ teachers compete in teams for a coveted prize. This is an excellent opportunity to learn more, hear directly from the UK universities and catch up with colleagues from other schools and colleges. There is an opportunity to attend various presentations, including a keynote address from the Chief Executive of UCAS and a wide range of breakout sessions to choose from. The UCAS Conference is particularly helpful if you want to meet the university recruitment teams on exhibition stands, ask them specific questions or invite them to visit your school. As with most conferences, it is a great place to source free pens, tote bags, soft toys and other university and UCAS-branded merchandise. Conference prices vary depending on whether you register for a residential package or a non-residential day delegate ticket.

Facebook is not known for the provision of impartial sources, but one bright spot is the 'UCAS Advisers' group run by Paul Teulon, who is a former Admissions Officer at the University of Oxford and King's College, London. Teulon rose to prominence through his careful analysis of the efficacy of intake qualifications while at King's College. The group is lively and full of good advice and timely reminders and warnings from experienced Advisers.

For Advisers, your everyday use of UCAS is on your UCAS Adviser Portal. For example, through 'Application Management' you can view student applications and their courses, upload references, manage and send your student's applications, and through 'Tracking offers and decisions' you can view the outcomes, offers and offer conditions. However, it's worth a pause here to mention a few things about UCAS, the charitable organisation based in Cheltenham:

- UCAS talks about their 'Journey to a Million', a prediction that in years to come, there will be over a million applicants in an application cycle. In 2023, over 750,000 students from the UK and across the globe applied, and over 550,000 began a course at a university or college in the UK.

- If you are interested in the governance and organisation, here is more information about **UCAS Council: https://www.ucas.com/about-us/who-we-are/corporate-governance/ucas-council**
- UCAS has a **Secondary Education Advisory Group**, with representatives from various schools and other organisations such as HELOA, the Career Development Institute and so on.
- UCAS reforms are important to follow, but it is not always obvious how to do this. You could read the TES or check on UCAS' news section of their website: https://www.ucas.com/corporate/news-and-key-documents/news

For example:

In 2022, seven questions were added to the UCAS application form to help universities with widening participation.

In 2023, the UCAS reference was reformed into three sections.

In 2024, UCAS shared the historical entry grades tool, which is a useful way to explore the relationship between the grades that represent typical offers and the grades achieved by students who begin on the course: https://www.ucas.com/undergraduate/applying-university/entry-requirements/understanding-historical-entry-grades-data.

The personal statement was recently reformed for candidates applying for 2026 university entry, which we discuss further in Chapter 6.

https://www.ucas.com/dashboard

The basics of UCAS for Advisers

All of the information you need for setting up UCAS for your school or college centre can be found on the UCAS website. Here, we offer a few insights into the application process, and in Chapter 6, we discuss the UCAS personal statement and the UCAS reference in Chapter 7.

Updating or changing information after UCAS submission

Try and ensure that all information is accurate and double-checked before you send a student's application to UCAS. Schools cannot change the reference or the predicted grades after an application has been sent to UCAS. Students have very limited scope to change information on their UCAS application, once it has been sent.

Students:

- Students cannot change their personal statement after their application has been sent to UCAS.

5| Managing University Applications: UK Focus

- Students can update certain details on the application form – for example, address, email and phone number – go to https://www.ucas.com/applying/after-you-apply/making-changes-your-application-after-you-apply
- For some changes, students need to complete an 'Update my details' form.
- Some specific changes can be made to qualifications via the 'Qualification Amendment Form'.
- If students decide to change a course, they must contact the university direct.
- A university choice can be 'substituted' within 14 days of the date on the welcome email.
- Students can add more choices (up to a maximum of five) if they did not use all five choices when they first applied.
- After submission, students can cancel or withdraw from a choice or cancel their whole application.

FAQs around the time when you submit the applications

- The 'Extra Activities' section on the UCAS application form is for UK students only and is not shown for international applicants.
- Staff management – make sure you have given permission to relevant staff to track applications; for example, Form Tutors may need access set up to see their Tutor Group's applications. You do this by clicking on 'Staff Management' and then adding any new staff members, who can then set up a UCAS account.
- https://www.ucas.com/search/frequently-asked-questions

How to enter qualifications - and how to set up UCAS so it has the ones for your school

- In your staff set up on UCAS, set up a qualification shortlist – add the qualifications used by your school; for example, A levels. You do this by going to 'Centre Management' for the correct year and then 'Add New' to the qualification shortlist. Ensure you have chosen correctly – GCSEs or IGCSEs, 9–1 or A*–G and so on.

Information about how students enter qualifications

Students should enter their pending qualifications and all achieved qualifications. Even if some of their GCSE grades may be lower than they had hoped for, it is important that they include every formal exam qualification they have taken, including re-sits.

- Students do this by first adding a Place of Education then adding qualification – make sure they have entered the correct date and exam board.

- For pending qualifications, students should add the grade as 'Pending' and then the school adds predicted grades.
- If you are checking GCSE or equivalent grades entered, you can tick the box to say 'Qualifications Checked' so that universities can see you have verified the qualifications. If you tick this box, it is essential that you check that the students' declared GCSE grades match with your school records. If you have new students who join your school or college in Year 12, consider how you will obtain, and who will record their Year 11 qualifications, so that you can verify these for any future UCAS applications or US university transcripts.

Students need to understand that when they have completed their part of the application, it has not been sent to UCAS; it is ready for the school to add their predicted grades and reference, finalise and then send. You can return the application to them so they can make subsequent changes, and only your school or college can send the application to UCAS.

Internal school/college deadlines and external UCAS deadlines

Depending on your cohort size, plan your internal school or college deadlines so that you can stay on target to process and send applications comfortably before the external deadlines set by UCAS. However, if you set the internal deadline too early, then teachers cannot write in enough depth and detail about students.

For example, if you have a large cohort of 100+ early applicants (for applicants to the University of Oxford and University of Cambridge and all applicants for Medicine, Veterinary Science and Dentistry), you could set a mid-September internal deadline for UCAS applications to be complete. This will make it possible to meet the external UCAS deadlines in mid-October and mid-January. Similarly, in order to keep your flow of work steady with sending UCAS applications before Christmas, you might set a mid-November internal deadline for all other UCAS applications with the January deadline.

The rationale here is to allow students flexibility and choose the deadline that will balance with their academic work and other commitments. For staff there is a benefit to spreading the workload, even though this results in a 'marathon' approach to the work required to support Year 13 students from September to January.

Deadlines imply 'everyone does everything hours before the deadline', and 'we simply cannot allow students to complete their applications at the last minute'. The trick is to make students feel they have complete flexibility while giving them very little (see staggered deadlines below). And there are good reasons for that; we don't want lots of stressed applicants, but we also need to avoid a scenario where all of our workload happens in the few days before the external deadline. Schools can only send UCAS applications *after* students have completed their part.

Nowadays, missing deadlines is of consequence at only some universities: Oxford, Cambridge and various medical schools and for Veterinary Science and Dentistry. The universities aren't obliged to consider an application if it is made after the January deadline, but some students may have pressing reasons. In a crisis, students can get away with a 'late application', beyond the equal consideration deadline in January.

Suggested plans and timelines

Here is an example of how you might stagger student deadlines, so they complete their UCAS applications according to when they would like your school or college to process and send their application. You could also suggest the same or similar staggered deadlines for the staff writing their UCAS references, to spread their workload.

- June – Year 12 teachers draft recommendations for students.
- September to January – students (now in Year 13) complete their UCAS application – see staggered deadlines.

	Internal school or college deadline for students and teachers	External UCAS deadline
UCAS 1: Students applying for Medicine, Veterinary Science and Dentistry	5 September	mid-October
UCAS 2: Students applying for Oxford and Cambridge	15 September	mid-October
UCAS 3: Students completing their UCAS in November	1 November	mid-January (check UCAS deadline date)
UCAS 4: Students completing their UCAS in December	1 December	mid-January (check UCAS deadline date)
UCAS 5: Students completing their UCAS in January	1 January	mid-January (check UCAS deadline date)

QUESTIONS TO CONSIDER

- When does your UK university preparation programme begin and end?
- What can your school or college do to help your students prepare for a UCAS application?

PRACTICAL TOOLS AND TIPS

From year group lists on a spreadsheet to Unifrog, there are various ways you can record and manage the applications your students are making. The challenge for schools is to develop, maintain and improve their own systems. Some examples of records you may want to keep include:

- your UCAS timeline, with internal and external deadlines;
- application portals;
- university admissions requirements;
- selection processes and admissions tests;
- applicant lists for UCAS, identifying students applying for early deadline courses;
- applicant lists for Gap Year students making a post-qualification application;
- university offers lists, recording the offer conditions and outcomes of applications;
- destinations lists, recording what students go on to do next.

Scenario

A student is applying for a highly competitive course such as single honours Computer Science at the University of Cambridge, Imperial, UCL, University of St Andrews and Durham University. The student is insistent on only applying to these 'aspirational' university choices. You advise them to include some 'solid' and 'safe' options, but they disagree, explaining that their parents will only allow them to enrol at one of those universities on their aspirational list. They have missed your internal deadlines, and you have one day left before the UCAS deadline, and your school is about to close for the October half-term. How will you advise them, and how will you respond?

Suggestions

You could send the UCAS application as it is, given the time constraints.

Alternatively, before you send it to UCAS, you may want reassurance from their Form Tutor or other relevant colleagues or contact their parents to make them aware of the high-stakes nature of this application. Find out if they have already registered to take any required admissions tests, as it is possible that they have missed the registration deadline for the TMUA required by the University of Cambridge. Are they also aware that Computer Science at Imperial requires the TARA test for 2026 entry?

If there is time, meet with the student and hear their voice to better understand the factors affecting their choices. Help the student to be reflective, and encourage them to look ahead to the different possible outcomes and consequences so they make their own informed decision, weighing up the opportunities with the risks. For example, how will they respond if they have no offers in January? Ask them if they have considered the admissions tests required and whether it is too late for them to register for these tests. If they are insistent on sticking with their combination of five highly competitive universities, talk to them about Clearing options. Discuss what their Plans B and C might be if their high-stakes Plan A doesn't work out.

> **Follow up**
>
> Use an appropriate method for recording your meeting with the student, such as a Unifrog interaction or similar. Consider writing a quick email to the student to record your conversation and summarise your advice and copy in relevant colleagues such as their Form Tutor or Head of Year and subject teacher. Maybe suggest solid and safer options for them to consider. Given the time constraints, give them a deadline for response. Maybe follow up with parents depending on what is appropriate, either by email or a phone call from you or their Form Tutor or Head of Year.

Supporting UK university applications

Consider how you might develop your UK university preparation to suit the needs of the students. Ask yourself what your school or college is trying to achieve. Where does UK university admission fit into your school or college mission? Here are examples of ways that you could support students:

- For Year 8 or Year 9, you could help them develop a range of academic and other interests and advise students making their GCSE choices.
- For Year 10 and Year 11, you could support them with their Sixth Form subject choices, discuss their post-16+ options, research into different careers, encourage them to organise work experience and help them to think positively about their futures.
- For Year 12, you could discuss their post-18+ options, including Degree Apprenticeships and advise university applicants on degree course choice and selection processes including personal statements, admissions tests and interviews. You could encourage them to do super-curricular activities and help them prepare to make a competitive university application (see suggestions in Chapter 2).
- For Year 13, you could advise them on how to complete their UCAS, how to make their Firm and Insurance choices, and cover student finance and booking accommodation.

> **PRACTICAL TOOLS AND TIPS**
>
> Once students have created a UCAS account and begun their application, schools can monitor the progress of applications on the 'Adviser Portal' and after they have been sent to UCAS, track the outcome of these applications.

Suggested plans and timelines

Arrange a UCAS Day for Year 12, ideally around June, when students and their Form Tutors are off the timetable and can support students with their applications.

Typically, the main aim of a day like this is to help an entire cohort of students to start their UCAS applications and start a draft version of their personal statement (see Chapter 6). However, there are many possible variations with the content and the timings, building in breaks and lunch or spreading this over two mornings (rather than a whole day) and different levels of staff involvement, from a small team delivering the whole day, to Form Tutors and Heads of Department being available to support students throughout the day.

In order to get students to the point where they will benefit from such a day, consider how and when your programme will need to start. For example, if Year 12 can be introduced to university admissions and start their UCAS research in January, by June, they will hopefully have a clearer idea about their course choice. Consider also how you will manage students who are undecided about courses or choosing between two different courses.

ACTIVITY

Plan a Higher Education Day for Year 12. Consider the needs of the whole year group and what you will focus on. Possibilities might include:

- the school or college library, books, journals and academic resources;
- invite alumni to speak on a panel and share their experience with current students;
- invite the Headteacher or Senior Leadership Team to address the cohort;
- invite a teacher to speak on the theme of the value of university study;
- consider drop-in sessions or a series of optional breakout sessions to tailor the day to the needs of different students;
- consider how different Heads of Department and teachers can support students to take part in super-curricular activities to support their applications.
- consider one-to-one meetings between students and their Form Tutor, so Form Tutors can draft their overall UCAS reference;
- a focus on admissions tests;
- a focus on university interviews.

Time	Student activity	Staff involved
Assembly	The plan for the day: an introduction	Staff organising the day
Morning session 1	Subject-specific personal statement workshop	With Heads of Department and relevant teachers
Morning session 2	Starting the UCAS application form	With Form Tutors and Head of Year
Keynote talk 1	Attend a presentation on a key theme such as student finance or the transition to university	Student recruitment representatives from universities
Afternoon session 1	Shortlisting UCAS courses using UCAS Hub or Unifrog	With Form Tutors and Head of Year
Lunch		
Afternoon session 2	Continuing the UCAS application form	With Form Tutors and Head of Year
Keynote talk 2	Staff who have recently attended university speak on a panel about their university experience and what to expect	Teachers and staff
Final assembly	Conclusion to the day with a summary of key messages and a forward looking view about the timeline and next steps in the application process	Staff organising the day

PRACTICAL TOOLS AND TIPS

Students can apply to up to five universities via UCAS, but they could apply to just one choice if they wanted to. However, the best strategy is for students to use all five choices. Thinking ahead, in May or June of Year 13, they can only select two offers to go forward: a Firm offer, typically with higher conditions, and an Insurance choice with lower offer conditions. Students should apply to universities with a range of requirements, including some with requirements that are below their predicted grades, given that meeting the minimum requirements does not guarantee an offer.

From longlist to shortlist: Choosing five UK universities

The best advice for students is to choose their course first and their universities second. The rationale for this approach is that it doesn't really matter *where* they study; *what* they study is more important. In short, they should be encouraged to apply for a subject that will hold their interest for the duration of the course. Once Year 12 students know their predicted grades (ideally by June), they can begin their selection of five universities.

Advising students applying for highly competitive courses and universities

All university applications are competitive, but the level of competition can vary. At the time of writing, certain degree courses are in very high demand, including Computer Science, Law and Psychology (among others). Medicine, Veterinary Science and Dentistry are all highly competitive, and in Chapter 6, we explore these further, focusing on personal statements. By contrast, there are so-called recruiting subjects such as Classics, Music, Modern Languages, Theology and so on.

Students can determine the level of competition for their course by the following:

- the typical ratio of applicants to places for the course they are applying for;
- the requirement of an admissions test;
- additional elements beyond the UCAS application, such as an interview, submitted written work or a portfolio.

Given the level of competition for places at very highly ranked institutions, including some of the London University Colleges, there is arguably no need to treat applications to the University of Oxford and University of Cambridge any differently from any other UCAS application. The only significant differences are that (1) these two universities have a mid-October deadline and (2) they typically require additional elements which could include an admissions test, submitted work and maybe an interview if shortlisted.

UCL had approximately 80,000 applications for 7,500 places in 2024 (with 26 applications per place for Computer Science, and 22 applications per place for Law).

PRACTICAL TOOLS AND TIPS

Unifrog has a shortlisting tool that allows students to search for courses and compare colleges. This is a useful way for students to have more context and information, such as the number of applicants and places available. Each college is described using three adjectives such as 'modern, friendly, big'. Students can filter and rank the colleges, selecting different criteria of their choice, from the availability of accommodation to the frequency of formal dinners.

QUESTIONS TO CONSIDER

How will you approach 'Oxbridge' applicants?

'Oxbridge' refers to the University of Oxford and the University of Cambridge. Our suggestion is not to use this word. It isn't a real word, and it can cause resentment in the majority of the cohort if they feel the Oxford and Cambridge applicants are treated differently or are more important than other applicants. Some of your best students might choose not to apply to either of these universities and the level of competition for places on some courses may be greater at other universities such as UCL. Ideally, all students in your cohort should be encouraged to put together a competitive application, do extension work and super-curricular activities (and if appropriate, prepare for admissions tests and interviews) regardless of where they are applying. Some schools will identify students as potential Oxford or Cambridge candidates and expect them to take part in a special 'Oxbridge class'. However, increasingly, this approach is problematic. Given that Imperial College London, the University of Warwick and Durham University require admissions tests and Medicine and Veterinary Sciences will require interviews, you may want your entire cohort to take part in a preparation or enrichment programme that will benefit them all and convey to every student that they are valued in this process by you.

Advising students applying for Medicine, Veterinary Science and Dentistry

For Medicine, Veterinary Science and Dentistry, the competition for places is understandably fierce, and students should think carefully about their four UCAS choices and their fifth related course choice. If you have students applying for one of these courses, consider how you can support them with different elements of the application and selection process that will include the following:

- the correct subjects at A level or IB;
- UCAT preparation;
- work experience and regular volunteering;
- personal statement (see Chapter 6);
- evidence of personal qualities, attributes and skills;
- interview preparation and mock interview practice.

Given the huge cost of training junior doctors, a robust process is needed for selecting medics. The Medic Portal comparison tool and other resources here come highly recommended: https://www.themedicportal.com

Students should also research into each of the medical schools they are applying to and understand their selection processes.

For example, Hull York Medical School: https://www.hyms.ac.uk/medicine/applying/selection-procedure

There are multiple routes into healthcare professions. Students considering Medicine should also consider these allied areas, from Nursing and Midwifery to Dental Hygienist, Optometry or Physiotherapy.

NHS Allied Health Professions:

https://www.healthcareers.nhs.uk/explore-roles/allied-health-professionals/roles-allied-health-professions
Medic Portal: https://www.themedicportal.com/application-guide/allied-health/

ACTIVITY

Plan a programme from Year 10 upwards for prospective medics, veterinary scientists and dentists. How will you encourage them to seek work experience and opportunities for volunteering?

Consider how you will manage the writing of UCAS references for students applying for these courses via UCAS (see Chapter 7).

Replying to UCAS offers, exam results and Clearing

Strategy is needed towards the end of the UCAS process. UCAS specifies a reply deadline for students, which depends on when the applicant receives all their offers. Students must reply to offers before their specified reply deadline, or their offers will be lost. They select two offers: a Firm choice and an Insurance choice.

Encourage students to think carefully about what would make a sensible Firm and Insurance choice. They should think carefully about their strategy and reply well before the UCAS reply deadline. The Insurance choice is not really the same as 'a second choice'. This is an important distinction, because strategy is needed, and the Insurance choice should be an offer with lower requirements.

The Firm choice should typically have higher offer conditions than the Insurance, and it should be a university they are prepared to go to. The purpose of a well-chosen Insurance choice is that the offer conditions are sufficiently lower than the Firm choice, which provides a secure backup option if they miss the offer conditions of their Firm choice. If universities don't accept students who have missed their offer conditions, they will be eligible for Clearing where they can look for alternative options. Eligible students may want to find a place using Clearing Plus, which automatically matches them to courses with vacancies.

Clearing https://www.ucas.com/undergraduate/clearing-and-results-day/what-clearing
Clearing Plus https://www.ucas.com/providers/our-products-and-services/student-recruitment-and-marketing/clearing-plus

Advising students about Firm and Insurance choices

Sound advice about Firm and Insurance choices is essential. Take time and plan for how you will advise Year 13 students who have received all their decisions. You could hold an assembly or group meetings in which you cover the information or, depending on the time available, you could also meet with them individually. The rationale here is to encourage them to make sensible, informed choices.

Encourage students to be open-minded. Help them strike a balance between being optimistic and realistic about their choices. Encourage them to be aspirational but also strategic. Ideally, at least two of their five university choices should be comfortably achievable and potential Insurance options. The Firm offer conditions should be higher than the Insurance conditions; if the Firm choice offer is A, A, A, it is better for the Insurance offer to be lower, such as A, B, B.

The 'received wisdom' is for Advisers to encourage students to limit their level of risk by picking an Insurance option with significantly lower requirements to avoid a scenario where 'too many' students in the year group miss the conditions of both of their UCAS offers. However, there is more nuance here: students should decide on their level of risk. If the aim of your students is to gain admission to the best possible university for their course, they may choose to take a risk on their Firm and Insurance choices, with a view to using Clearing if needed. Clearing is a popular and respected way to find a university place and the closest we have to 'post-qualification' university admissions.

Before they make their Firm and Insurance choices, your generic advice could cover these points:

- The Insurance choice should have lower offer conditions than the Firm offer conditions.
- They can only reply to their UCAS offers in one sitting.
- They must reply to offers before the deadline set.
- They cannot switch their Firm and Insurance choices, so they should only reply to the offers once they have decided.
- Consider visiting or attending an offer holder Open Day, and do more research into their course, the data available and so on.
- They should take their time before they decide on which university offers they want to accept as their Firm and Insurance options.
- They may want to attend offer holder Open Days, and do further research, comparing their courses.
- Students may want to take a risk on their Firm and Insurance choice, or they may prefer to limit the level of risk by choosing a 'safe' Insurance option.
- Clearing is their back up option, and Clearing Plus will automatically match eligible students to suitable university courses.

QUESTIONS TO CONSIDER

- What data and information can help students make informed choices?
- Staff who are involved in Results Day for the first time may be anxious. What can you do to help them prepare and plan ahead?
- Schools can help advise, but students reflect on the level of risk they are prepared to take. How can you encourage them to make their own informed decisions about their Firm and Insurance choices?

UCAS advice on Firm and Insurance choices:

https://www.ucas.com/applying/after-you-apply/types-undergraduate-offers/replying-your-ucas-undergraduate-offers

UCAS Track during July and August

During the summer months, students may usually check their status on UCAS Track. However, Track is closed during two week-long embargo periods in order for UCAS to process exam results. These dates will vary from year to year, but as an example, these were the two embargo periods in 2024:

- Monday, 29 July 18:00–Tuesday, 6 August 09:00
- Friday, 9 August 14:00–Thursday, 15 August 07:00

If students narrowly miss their conditional offers, they may want to check their status on UCAS Track to find out if their application has been made 'Unsuccessful' or 'Unconditional'. This is likely to fall during the staff holiday when students' anxieties might be increasing at home. This raises a question about how you might support students who need advice during the summer months when your school or college is closed.

Supporting students who miss their conditional offers

Schools and colleges need to decide what level of support and advice they will offer after students have left school. A policy on this is ideal, so students and parents know what to expect after Year 13 exam results are published, which is also when schools are usually closed for the summer holidays.

International Baccalaureate Diploma Programme students have time in July to consider options in Clearing, as their results are published on 6 July, which coincides with the start of UCAS Clearing. A level Results Day in mid-August is when eligible students will be looking for a course in Clearing.

Increasingly, universities don't welcome correspondence from schools following the release of exam results. Some schools write supporting letters for students who have narrowly missed offer conditions, hoping that will give them a chance of securing the place. Others will be available to advise students who have missed offers. Students need to be proactive if they are hoping to find a place in Clearing. Clearing Plus automatically matches a student with university courses with vacancies. You could set up an FAQ page for Clearing and post-results advice or be available for consultation with students at set times. Students are usually pleasantly surprised by the range of courses available in Clearing.

> **QUESTIONS TO CONSIDER**
>
> - How will you respond and what will your school or college do if a student misses their UK university offer conditions?
> - Will a team of staff be available to advise students?
> - Will you meet with students and/or their parents and guardians?
> - Will you encourage students to write a letter of continued interest to the university where they have missed the offer conditions?
> - How will you communicate with students about their other options or alternatives/next steps, including Clearing and so on?

> **PRACTICAL TOOLS AND TIPS**
>
> - Pick 20+ courses and universities in Clearing that your students are likely to be interested in. Use a whiteboard or equivalent to show your most popular university courses and their entry requirements in Clearing so students can see this information at a glance.
> - Your experience of the courses available in Clearing and the typical entry conditions year on year will help inform the following admissions cycle next year. For example, in recent years, A100 Medicine has been available at St George's, University of London.
> - Note and record the courses in Clearing and their entry conditions for reference. You can share your list of students who gain places via Clearing with staff and senior leaders to show that Clearing is a viable way to gain entry to university.

How to set up and manage an advice service for students on exam Results Day

Students typically know their university decisions on UCAS Track before they receive their exam results. Questions to consider:

1. Who is available to advise students on Results Day?
2. What physical spaces in school can you use? Do you need a more private area for students who are upset? Are there individual offices or meeting rooms for individual discussions between Advisers and students and maybe their parents, guardians or carers?

3. How will you communicate information about your Results Day service in advance? Do you need an FAQ page set up on your school website?
4. How and when will students receive their exam results?
5. How will you communicate with students on the day? What will you plan for? Will you need a booking system? Will you meet students in person? Do you need an alternative option for students to communicate via a phone call, online meeting or email?
6. How will you allocate staff to students who request individual advice? How will you manage multiple enquiries on the day?
7. What do you need to do before the day? For example, find out which universities prefer to use a Clearing form online versus which universities use a phone line.

> **Scenario**
>
> Following the publication of Year 13 exam results in August, you receive multiple enquiries from parents and students. You also receive an email from the Assistant Head reminding you that, due to GDPR, you should only respond to queries from students. How do you handle these scenarios and respond to these various emails? The emails consist of different types of requests:
>
> 1. Parent A wants to discuss the exam results and asks for information about the process for re-marking exam papers.
> 2. Parent B seeks information about UCAS Clearing options for students who missed both their Firm and Insurance university offers.
> 3. Parent C asks for a meeting with you to discuss whether their daughter should take up her university place for September or take a Gap Year, and reapply for entry in the following year.
> 4. Parent D contacts you to say that despite his son having been predicted A, A, B, he secured A*, A*, A, the grades that could have secured him a place at his first-choice university. Their son didn't receive offers from the University of Oxford or UCL and the parent wants to discuss this with the school.
>
> How do you respond to these scenarios? By letter, email, phone call or more than one of these three – or not at all?

Suggestions

1. Information about the re-marks process can be sent by email or through an FAQ page that covers typical questions. Send them the information and mention that if they still have questions, they should let you know.
2. If the student is over 18, you might prefer to contact the student directly and inform the parent that the student has the relevant information needed. It is your responsibility to ensure that the students have access to the relevant information, which is also easily accessible on the UCAS website. Generic information about UCAS Clearing can be drafted and sent to parents and students as an FAQ-type generic response in advance. You could also plan ahead by covering this information in an assembly.
3. During the school holidays, you might not be contracted to work. However, if you are, you could suggest a virtual meeting online or a phone call. This is a time-sensitive question. If the student is taking up a place at university, they will need to decide around mid-August. If they aren't taking up a university place, it could be quickly reallocated by the university concerned via Clearing.
4. You need the school's UCAS predictions policy on hand and data about the school's prediction accuracy in general (from previous cycles). A discussion of either re-marks or exam grades could fall outside the job description for the staff responsible for supporting students with their university applications, in which case direct this email back to a senior member of staff or a relevant colleague who is responsible for academic matters. However, if this is within your remit, you need to deal with it. Keep a copy of your predictions policy (which you can send to parents in Year 12) and record data for each application cycle that provides evidence of the accuracy of your predicted grades. Offer to speak to their son. Congratulate the student on their excellent grades and be ready to discuss their options. Find out if they want to reapply to, for example, the University of Oxford or UCL, and focus on advising their son on his next steps. If needed, have information ready about making a new UCAS application. If they decide to reapply to Oxford and UCL, mention that these excellent grades do not guarantee an offer, given the competitive nature of the application process and the various elements of an application, which could include a university admissions test or interview. Outline the timeline and support available for students who have left the school.

> **QUESTIONS TO CONSIDER**
> - Consider if students who have left can still apply via the school. Who will be able to advise them and when?
> - Will you support your so-called 'Year 14' students, also known as post-qualification applicants (PQA)?
> - What will be your policy for students who have left your institution and request your support with a new application or request documents such as updated references or academic transcripts?

Understanding fee code

Students might ask you for advice determining their fee code. Students are required to indicate how they will pay their tuition fees on their UCAS application.

At English universities, UK students pay 'home fees', which were £9,250 per year from 2017, increasing to £9,535 for 2025 entry. International students (from outside the EU, Switzerland and EEA) normally pay considerably more, and the amount varies from one university to another and from one course to another. The average is around £18,000 per year for tuition fees.

Fees for Scottish students are around £1,800 per year. It is free for students who are eligible, but they need to apply for each year of study to the Student Awards Agency Scotland (SAAS), which assesses student finance applications and pays bursaries for students from Scotland. Students who are not eligible must pay.

Undergraduate funding in Scotland: https://www.saas.gov.uk/full-time/undergraduates

On the UCAS form, students state their nationality, residency status and how they plan to fund their studies. Universities determine a student's fee status according to (1) nationality or whether they have 'settled' status or 'indefinite leave to remain' in the UK and (2) where their ordinary residence has been for the three years before they start university.

For more information on fee status: https://www.ukcisa.org.uk/Information--Advice/Fees-and-Money/England-HE-fee-status

Expectations, student finance, costs and graduate employment

There are multiple factors influencing students: finance, costs, fees, loans, proximity, distance from home and perceived prestige of options and institutions. Students should not be put off going to university by the costs; loans are available, and earning money while at university is possible. Students from England will not need to repay their tuition fee loan until they are earning over a threshold of £25,000 (thresholds for other UK countries vary). The comparison often made is that this is more like a graduate tax, and so money shouldn't be an obstacle to funding university. However, given that the true cost of a UK university education, over three or four years, including tuition fees, maintenance and living expenses, and accommodation, totals approximately £100,000, it cannot be assumed that all students will want to take on these loans. However, despite the financial concerns and competition for graduate jobs, on average graduates earn more over their lifetime. Furthermore, it is difficult to quantify the true value of a degree and the significant benefits in terms of personal and intellectual development.

> **PRACTICAL TOOLS AND TIPS**
>
> Media outlets and news articles list UK degree courses in relation to graduate salaries.
>
> Students can see the data for their chosen course, including the average earnings of graduates: https://discoveruni.gov.uk
>
> An annual report by High Fliers Research into graduate employment may also be of interest to students. It shows important trends and data that might inform students when choosing their degree course and university, for example, which universities are most targeted by graduate employers: https://www.highfliers.co.uk

Context and statistics

Graduate employment

There are around 750,000 applicants to UK universities and around 640,000+ entrants in a typical year. University students drop out in significant numbers, with only around 500,000 completing their degree course. They then face fierce competition for a graduate job. The top 100 employers have around 28,500 vacancies, and there are only 35,000 graduate programmes (top 100 plus others).

> **QUESTIONS TO CONSIDER**
>
> - How can you help students prepare for the intense competition shown by these statistics?
> - How do you advise students when things don't go to plan?
> - What can you do to educate your students about the costs and the loans available for tuition fees and maintenance? How might students evaluate the positives and negatives of fees being repaid once they are earning over a certain threshold?

Useful links

UK

- Choosing A level subjects and equivalent, published by the Russell Group https://www.informedchoices.ac.uk
- UCAS and Clearing https://www.ucas.com/undergraduate/clearing-and-results-day/check-availability-ucas-undergraduate-applications
- UCAS Gold, Silver and Bronze packages and reports https://www.ucas.com/advisers/managing-applications/upgrade-your-insight-additional-reports
- UCAS register your centre https://www.ucas.com/advisers/getting-started-adviser/becoming-ucas-centre
- UCAS reports https://www.ucas.com/data-and-analysis/undergraduate-statistics-and-reports/ucas-reports
- UCAS Toolkits for schools https://www.ucas.com/advisers/guides-resources-and-training/tools-and-resources-help-you

Student finance

- https://www.gov.uk/apply-online-for-student-finance
- https://www.gov.uk/government/publications/student-loans-a-guide-to-terms-and-conditions/student-loans-a-guide-to-terms-and-conditions-2023-to-2024
- https://www.gov.uk/repaying-your-student-loan/what-you-pay

Looking ahead: Key takeaways and questions to consider

- *Students.* **Successful university applications require research, strategy, planning and preparation.** How do you encourage students to conduct thorough research? How might they decide between the course on offer and the perceived reputation of the university? How can they use all five UCAS choices strategically?

- *Staff.* **Developing comprehensive university application support with structured application guidance is key.** How will you effectively support students from diverse backgrounds with different needs? How will you provide whole-year group information and personalised advice? How will you manage your exam Results Day and post-results support? How might you allocate time for students so you can support them with a Firm and Insurance strategy for their UCAS choices?

- *Senior Leaders.* **Allocating the necessary resources and investing in staff training are vital to ensure students have accurate, relevant and high-quality advice and support.** How can your school or college management structures ensure that effective guidance takes place across the school?

6 | Supporting personal statements: UCAS focus

The personal statement, written by the student, needs to demonstrate their interest in and suitability for their chosen course. This chapter focuses on how to support students in writing their UCAS personal statements, which for 2026 university entry has been 'reformed' to include three questions. For UK university admissions, choosing a course is very important. Given that a personal statement is a student's pitch for their suitability for a course, a decision is needed about the course they are applying for. Students should research the course so they are familiar with the content, structure and assessment for the duration of the degree.

This chapter will cover:

- staffing: building a team and utilising all available resources;
- 'Subject-specific Advisers' and 'Careers Champions';
- an overview of UCAS personal statements;
- the writing process: planning, drafting and finalising;
- the three sections of the personal statement with suggested prompts;
- processing UCAS applications, and timelines and deadlines;

Staffing: Building a team and utilising all available resources

Excellent university applications are not written by the careers department; they result from the applicant and UCAS references which include relevant input from multiple teachers. Consider how you will prepare students so they can make a competitive UCAS application. It is important to have the correct level of staffing, a topic we discussed in Chapter 4. Teachers and other staff may be willing to help students with the various elements – feedback on personal statements and drafting UCAS references, but also preparation for university admissions tests, mock interviews and so on.

However, staff get busy, so try to inspire them to take an interest in their students' university applications. Make sure that staff know the students they are mentoring, allowing or giving extra time for the meetings and writing of the UCAS reference. For example, one 'covered lesson' per pupil supported might not cover the exact time given, but it is an acknowledgement that this is a role that does take time. Additional support might be needed from support staff or where pupils have Special Education Needs (SEN) or have had a history of behavioural and/or emotional issues.

Over the years, we have developed several strategies that include staff helping in a number of ways:

- A Higher Education Day for Year 12 in June when staff are available to support students applying for different subject areas.
- Subject teachers draft recommendations that are used in UCAS references, which we cover in more detail in Chapter 7.
- Teachers share their subject-specific knowledge to support students with their personal statements, admissions tests and mock interviews.
- Developing staff with expertise who can support students with UCAS applications outside traditional academic departments in our school or college. A group of subject-specific Advisers could support students with UCAS applications in a particular degree area, for example, Architecture, Engineering, Medicine and Law (if you don't offer Law at A level or equivalent). An alternative idea might be to look to parents or governors of the school for this kind of subject specialism, who can volunteer their time to support specific elements of the application, such as a parent who is a doctor volunteering to help prepare students for Medicine interviews.

'Subject-specific Advisers' and 'Careers Champions'

Heads of Department or Advisers for a particular subject can play a key role in supporting students applying for particular subjects. For example, they could run workshops and offer students subject-specific feedback on their personal statements.

Subject-specific expertise is important. In schools where careers are embedded in the curriculum, these staff are sometimes known as 'Careers Champions', the member of staff in each academic department who has taken responsibility for careers or university guidance as their project. This role might also include expertise in related degree courses and supporting students with writing personal statements in that subject.

Consider how you might resource support for popular subject areas with large numbers of applicants such as Computer Science, Psychology or Economics. It is also important to support applicants applying for degrees outside your teaching curriculum, such as Medicine or

Engineering. Staff with a degree in a particular area that is not taught at school might want to take this on as a special role. For example:

- an English teacher who has a Law degree could be an Adviser for Law;
- a Maths teacher who studied Economics at university could be an Adviser for Economics, Business and Management;
- a Physics teacher who is an engineering undergraduate could become an Adviser for Engineering, related STEM subjects and so on; or
- a Geography teacher could develop a specialism for supporting applicants for Geography, International Relations, Human Social and Political Sciences, or Land Economy.

An overview of UCAS personal statements

The clue is in the title: *personal* statement. Students write it, so it is up to them to get on with it. By contrast, schools write academic references (UCAS references are covered in Chapter 7 and US references in Chapter 9), and these are the documents that are your responsibility. The UCAS reference is an essential part of the UCAS application process; it reinforces the pupil's personal statement. A student's motivation to pursue a course might be quite personal. For example, they want to do Psychology because they have had mental health struggles of their own, and this generally makes for quite an interesting start.

In terms of your time, focus and attention, get the balance right and consider how you can help students keep it in perspective. The personal statement is a short piece of writing (no more than 4,000 characters) compared with other assignments that Year 12 students are familiar with.

However, there are potential pitfalls. Some parents and students may expect a level of support and amount of feedback that is unrealistic. The solution here is to communicate and share relevant information and advice. Check UCAS guidance, which is clear and comprehensive. Tactfully set out expectations and develop policies based on UCAS guidance and communicate this via letters. Set internal deadlines, and send reminders and updates to students and parents, as appropriate.

Consider the basic information about personal statements and when you will convey this. It is an opportunity for a student to differentiate themself from other applicants. This is the part of the application that the student writes and is responsible for, and so the role of the school or college is only to ensure that the relevant information, advice and support are well-timed and appropriate. Introducing basic information about the personal statement around the middle of Year 12 will allow students enough time to think carefully about the course they might apply for in Year 13, and what they might include in their writing.

The personal statement is typically part of the selection process. Universities 'make use' of it in various ways, and it can make the difference between an offer and a rejection, hence the need for clear information and appropriate support. The personal statement is the one opportunity that students have to articulate why they are suitable for their chosen course. Whatever their preferred degree course for UK universities, students are best advised to apply for the same course across their five universities; they can only write one personal statement so it needs to 'fit' for all of their choices. It is a student's elevator pitch.

The writing process: Planning, drafting and finalising

Encourage students to get on with planning, drafting and finalising their personal statement. But as this is their writing, it is not for staff to spend time chasing or cajoling them to finish it. Let them own it: the writing process and the finished piece. The best advice is to help them get started early on a draft. Students often find it hard to know where to start; encourage them to write bullet points and then shape this into sentences and paragraphs. They often find the idea of writing about themselves 'cringey'; a bullet point list of what they have done and why they want to do the course can overcome this hesitancy. One piece of helpful advice is that 're-writing is writing'. Making mistakes, redrafting, experimenting and polishing; this is the craft of writing.

Teachers have subject-specific expertise; they know their subject and what counts as accurate subject content. Teachers can benefit students with their expertise in their subject area and related degree courses.

PRACTICAL TOOLS AND TIPS

Unifrog's personal statement tool allows students to request feedback from their teachers. We would recommend that students avoid multiple rounds of feedback from staff. It is their work, and feedback should be limited to one or two relevant staff, such as a Head of Department, a subject-specific teacher or the student's Form Tutor. Communicate clearly to staff, parents and students that this should not be taking up a lot of staff time; this is a personal statement written by the student, and it should be their initiative. The end of Year 12 and the start of Year 13 is a vital time to teach the syllabus and give opportunities for assessment with accurate marking and feedback to ensure the results are as good as they can be by the end of Year 13. Teachers taking too much time on personal statement feedback could impede all this good work and put unnecessary pressure on students at this time of the academic year.

The three sections of the personal statement with suggested prompts

For the 2026 university entry, UCAS has reformed the personal statement to include three 'scaffolded' questions, which makes the task even clearer for students. Scaffolding implies support provided for all students. The three key questions UCAS now proposes to use are the kind of questions and prompts Unifrog and schools would have used in the past to plan and shape a good personal statement.

The total of 4,000 characters (which includes spaces), and each of the three sections has a minimum of 350 characters. Students write a response to these three specific questions set by UCAS, and for each we have added some prompts. Inevitably, schools will continue to advise and guide on what is and is not appropriate for each section, with some suggestions below.

Question 1: Why do they want to study this course or subject?

This question invites an explanation from students. However, explanations can vary; there are different types of explanations; explaining 'why' implies an answer that 'because . . .' In this context, 'because' relates to why they want to study the course they are applying for. They could consider the 'past', 'present' and 'future', starting with what first sparked their interest. How and when did it begin, what interests them now, and consider how this links to their future? Here they are explaining why, in terms of their personal motivation to study the subject and how that began.

- What can they bring to the course in terms of interest, motivation, skills or a new perspective?
- How does the course they are applying for link to their plans for the future or any ideas about a career they might pursue?

They might think about different types of reasons, personal reasons, either how their interest began or longer-term or career-related reasons or their interest in the course itself. Arguably, admissions tutors are more interested in the latter, in what they have to say about the course and subject content; their suitability for what lies ahead, and so their interest in modules and topics is more appropriate than lengthy accounts of when their childhood interest was first sparked.

- Research into the course content online, which they can find on UCAS or the university websites: What interests them about the course they are applying for?
- Considering the duration of the whole course from Year 1 onwards, what are the topics or modules they are looking forward to most and why? Year 1 could be generic or similar across universities; it is Years 2 and 3 that show specialism and reflect the differences in the courses.

- Are there any optional or core/compulsory modules that interest them and why?
- Does the course include something distinctive that they might mention, such as a placement year/a year in industry/study abroad?
- Give any other reasons or further explanation of why they are applying for this course.

The advice is to apply for the same course across all five UCAS choices because students can only write one personal statement. There is significant variation across degree courses as to how far personal statements play a role in the selection of candidates, but students should ensure that their personal statement is relevant for each course they are applying to.

Higher Education Policy Institute article on use of personal statements:

https://www.hepi.ac.uk/2023/06/15/how-do-admissions-professionals-use-the-ucas-personal-statement-2/

The University of Durham will accept a substitute personal statement for students who may be applying for a course that is different from their other UCAS choices.

https://www.durham.ac.uk/study/undergraduate/how-to-apply/writing-a-personal-statement/

Students can check each university policy on their entry criteria and how their personal statement will be used in the selection process. For example, the University of Bristol specifies if and when the personal statement could be used to differentiate between applicants, depending on the course they are applying to:

https://www.bristol.ac.uk/study/undergraduate/apply/admissions-statements/

Question 2: How have their qualifications and studies helped them to prepare for this course or subject?

This question invites them to describe 'how' their Year 12/13 studies have prepared them for their university course. There's a link to be made between what they are studying now and what they would like to study in the future. Arguably, this question may be more challenging for degree courses outside of traditional curriculum areas, such as Engineering, Architecture or Medicine. If they are applying for one of these, think about how they can demonstrate their interest and focus on the most relevant subjects and their skills.

- How has their curriculum prepared them for university study?
- How do their (A level, IBDP, IBCP, T level, BTEC or equivalent) subjects link to the course they are applying for?

- What skills do they have that make them suitable for the course?
- Do they have any relevant research skills, for example, an EPQ or IB Extended Essay?
- Include any other relevant examples from their studies to show their suitability for the course.
- What super-curricular activities have they done that demonstrate their interest (see Chapter 2)? Have they done reading, podcasts, lectures, research, taster days, extension classes or any other relevant activities outside the classroom?
- What further examples or evidence can they use from their education to show that they are suited to the course they are applying for?

Question 3: What else have they done to prepare outside of education, and why are these experiences useful?

This question invites them to describe 'what' and explain 'why'. There's space here for them to mention anything else that they want admissions tutors to know about what they have done to prepare.

- What are their personal interests, and hobbies and how might these be relevant in their application?
- Consider activities and experiences that they have done outside of lessons: volunteering, clubs or other activities, such as sports, music, drama and so on.
- How might their work experience, internships or experiences of the workplace be relevant?

ACTIVITY

- Research into the course content for International Management at the University of Bath, focusing on the topics they will cover and the skills they need to succeed in this course;

  https://www.bath.ac.uk/courses/undergraduate-2025/business-and-management/bsc-international-management-with-study-or-work-abroad/

- Compare this with the equivalent degree course at the University of Warwick and UCL and think about the similarities and differences between these three courses:

  https://warwick.ac.uk/study/undergraduate/courses/bsc-international-management/
  https://www.ucl.ac.uk/prospective-students/undergraduate/degrees/international-management-bsc

- If they are writing a personal statement for International Management, consider how they might focus on the common themes and topics covered in all courses.

PRACTICAL TOOLS AND TIPS

Good advice for students is to think **Activity, Benefit, Course** (ABC):

- **Activity.** What have they done to demonstrate their suitability or interest?
- **Benefit.** So what? What relevant insights or experience have they gained?
- **Course.** How does this link to the course they are applying for?

Check to see the specific personal statement guidance for the courses or the university they are applying to, for example, University of Bath:

https://www.bath.ac.uk/guides/writing-a-personal-statement-for-an-undergraduate-course/

Course focus. Look closely at the course content, and identify the topics and areas in common so that they can link their interests to the course content.

Skills focus. Identify the skills needed to succeed on the course they are applying for. In what ways can they demonstrate that they already have some of these skills?

QUESTIONS TO CONSIDER

Consider how and when you will do the following:

- communicate the relevant information about personal statements to students;
- provide an appropriate level of support for students;
- manage and track the progress of students' personal statements;
- ensure that students stay on track with meeting internal and external deadlines.

> **PRACTICAL TOOLS AND TIPS**
>
> Think carefully about how students can convey their suitability. There's a dilemma if they are applying for different courses across their five UCAS choices. For example, Philosophy, Politics and Economics at three choices and Philosophy and Economics at two other universities will be straightforward. However, if they are applying for very different courses they may need to select a narrower range of courses with more obvious overlap. There are some exceptions, for example applicants for the UCL BASc degree might struggle to write a personal statement that shows their interest in the Arts and Sciences degree course and their other UCAS choices, hence they send eligible applicants a questionnaire instead.
>
> For Medicine, they should research into what is required on a personal statement, including a focus on personal attributes, skills and reflection on work experience and volunteering.
>
> https://www.themedicportal.com/application-guide/personal-statement/

Processing UCAS applications, timelines and deadlines

In Year 12, students research into university courses and begin a draft personal statement. From the first term of Year 13 the applications are sent. It is useful for schools and colleges to have a list of students interested in applying to courses with an early deadline (Oxford or Cambridge, or for Medicine, Veterinary Science and Dentistry), ideally by the end of Year 12. If schools have an approximate number, they can plan to process students' applications for the early deadline, **15 October** and the regular deadline on **14 January**.

> **PRACTICAL TOOLS AND TIPS**
>
> Consider how to communicate information and advice to students about personal statements:
>
> - choose the university course first;
> - choose the universities second;
> - draft and finalise their personal statement;
> - prepare for and take admissions tests, and send submitted work (if needed).

As suggested in Chapter 5, a Higher Education Day around June or July, which allows students to get their UCAS applications off to a good start, could include subject-specific personal statement workshops in different subjects. Overall, this saves time so you don't have to repeat the same information to every student over and over again. Also, the summer is a good time as teachers will have more time when they are no longer teaching Years 11 and 13 once they are taking exams.

Suggested plans and timelines

An example of a timeline for UCAS

	Student activities	**Staff activities**
Year 12 Term 1	Introduce your programme and all of the post-18 options. For UK university applications, focus on how to choose a course. Encourage students to think about activities that will enhance an application and start working on this as work experience placements can take time.	Introductory assembly and follow up with emails and reminders.
Year 12 Term 2	Research courses and complete searches using UCAS Hub and/or Unifrog if available. Do specific research into course content. Begin a draft personal statement.	Introduce basic information about the personal statement in an assembly. Share resources with students and encourage them to begin a draft version.
Year 12 Term 3	Organise a Higher Education Day with time allocated to start a UCAS application and time to refine their draft personal statement.	Feedback on personal statement for early applicants to Oxford, Cambridge, Medicine, Veterinary Science and Dentistry. If available, relevant teachers could offer subject-specific advice or feedback. Subject teachers produce draft material for references.

6| Supporting Personal Statements

	Student activities	Staff activities
Year 13 Term 1	For UCAS October deadline: Complete all sections of UCAS application including personal statement final version – by the internal deadline, in early or mid-September. For UCAS January deadline: Complete all sections of UCAS application – by mid-November.	Feedback on personal statement for other UCAS applicants. Form Tutors or UCAS mentors collate information and produce a final draft reference.
Year 13 Term 2	Decide on Firm and Insurance choices and reply to offers before the deadline set by UCAS.	Send UCAS applications before the equal consideration deadline in mid-January.
Year 13 Term 3	Apply for student finance and book accommodation.	Check that students have replied to their offers. Send email reminders via UCAS Track and ensure that they respond before their reply deadlines.

Useful links

For further information, check UCAS resources for students:

- UCAS guidance on personal statements https://www.ucas.com/applying/applying-to-university/writing-personal-statement/how-write-personal-statement
- UCAS personal statement reform https://www.ucas.com/about-us/news-and-insights/reforming-admissions
- UCAS Toolkit for Advisers https://www.ucas.com/advisers/toolkits
- Unifrog guidance on personal statements https://www.unifrog.org/know-how/how-to-write-your-personal-statement-like-a-boss

Looking ahead: Key takeaways and questions to consider

- *Staff.* **The personal statement is an important part of the selection process at most universities and for various courses.** How will you coordinate subject-specific support for students writing their personal statement?
- *Students.* **The personal statement is an opportunity for students to express why they are suitable for the course they are applying for.** How might they plan, draft and finalise their complete personal statement?

7 | Writing university references: UCAS focus

This chapter focuses on the UCAS reference. We discuss references for UK university applications, including the information needed, the drafting and finalising of references, the timeframe and the deadlines.

This chapter will cover:

- predicted grades and understanding the selection process;
- UCAS references: what staff need to know;
- understanding the three sections of the UCAS reference;
- extenuating circumstances letters and forms;
- drafting factual and evidence-based statements;
- references and communicating predicted grades;
- the application process: checking and sending to UCAS.

Predicted grades and understanding the selection process

A UCAS application for a student in Year 13 requires a school or college to enter predicted grades. The UCAS reference and the predicted grades are both the responsibility of the school or college. Given that the student does not 'see' either of these elements of the application from their side, you will need to have policies in place to protect and clarify the responsibilities of teachers and staff who play a key role in drafting UCAS references and predicting a student's grades. It is a question of school policy regarding:

- whether, how and when students are informed about their UCAS predictions, and
- if and how the contents of their UCAS reference will be shared with them.

An Educator's Guide to University Applications

> **QUESTIONS TO CONSIDER**
>
> - UCAS references: Who is responsible for writing this document? What role do teachers play? Which teachers draft material? Who collates and finalises the school/college reference?
> - UCAS application: Who is responsible for finalising and sending the UCAS application?

UCAS has guidance for Advisers, for example, updates on the expectations of the school reference with a focus on factual, evidence-based statements. UCAS guidance specifies that predicted grades should be 'aspirational but achievable'. Schools and colleges need robust processes in place to justify and communicate these to students and parents, and the timing of this communication is important.

Students should be aware of the elements of the selection process, which could include any combination of the following: their personal statement, admissions tests, submitted work, portfolios, interviews and so on. Every university publishes its minimum academic requirements, such as A, A, B for A level or 38 IB points. However, meeting the minimum requirements does not guarantee an offer.

It is useful to give students their predicted grades at the end of Year 12 because this gives them time over the summer to further consider their five UCAS choices. Some schools offer the chance to raise the predicted grade on the basis of further tests or other evidence from early in Year 13, which may work as an incentive for students to focus on their studies over the summer break. Other schools take a very different approach and do not re-test students in September for very good reasons; predicted grades made at the end of Year 12, in June or July, are not the starting point for negotiation. UCAS is very clear that schools should have professional integrity and challenge parents and students who think that if they push hard enough, they will 'get the grades' they want. The predicted grade is the best estimate made by the teacher, based on their professional judgement. Your role should be to hold a line with parents and support teaching staff and their professional opinion.

QUESTIONS TO CONSIDER

- When and how students will receive their predicted grades?
- How will your school or college communicate these to parents and students?
- How might you offer students advice and support following the release of their predicted grades? Will you offer them a meeting with an HE Adviser? If you use Unifrog, will you send them reminders about tools and resources to help shortlist their UCAS choices?

PRACTICAL TOOLS AND TIPS

- Students need to know their predicted grades before they can finalise their UCAS shortlist.
- It is advisable that students are aware of their predictions, ideally towards the end of Year 12, so they can use the end of the Summer Term and the holidays to identify which are their 'aspirational', 'solid' and 'safe' choices.
- The UCAS guidelines specify that predicted grades are 'aspirational but achievable'. Predictions are typically the responsibility of academic staff or Heads of Department. It is important that the appropriate staff are ready to have conversations about managing expectations and ensure that predicted grades are reliable and robust.
- It is useful to have statistics on your predicted grades' accuracy. For example, a statement such as: 'In 2024 65% of our Year 13 students obtained grades that were the same as their predictions or better. It was 75% in 2023, and 70% in 2022.'

UCAS guidance on predicted grades:

https://www.ucas.com/advisers/help-and-training/guides-resources-and-training/application-overview/predicted-grades-what-you-need-know-entry-year

> **Scenario**
>
> You receive an email from a parent asking for a meeting to discuss their daughter's progress in Year 12 and university choices. They are asking to discuss their daughter's predicted grades and asking if their extenuating circumstances in Year 12 have been taken into account. They request a meeting with you and the Head of Sixth Form. How will you respond?

> **Suggestions**
>
> There are various elements to unpack and consider here:
>
> - Predicted grades: check them first, and check your policy on predictions.
> - Advice given by colleagues in previous years: try and find out what advice was given.
> - Consider a polite and quick follow up along these lines: thanking them for the email, suggesting a meeting and that you are liaising with relevant colleagues.
> - Arrange the meeting, in person or online, liaise with the relevant staff in advance, and consider if a member of the Senior Leadership Team can be present.
> - Before the meeting, prepare by summarising the advice you can give regarding their course choice and their university options based on the grades already predicted by their teachers.
> - Have the extenuating circumstances been taken into account? Should they be? Might the extenuating circumstances be included in Section 2 of the UCAS reference?

> **QUESTIONS TO CONSIDER**
>
> - How will your school or college manage and respond to the queries that students and parents might have about their predicted grades?
> - Who are the suitable staff members that can manage expectations?

UCAS references: What staff need to know

The UCAS reference gives the school's view of the student. It is a piece of writing in three structured sections that is read by course selectors and admissions tutors who are responsible for making a decision about the application. The UCAS reference outlines a student's suitability and academic potential for the course they are applying for, allowing the universities to make a decision about their application. The reference can demonstrate how the student is performing compared with their peers in their cohort, their academic commitment and any relevant extenuating circumstances that may have affected their education or academic achievement.

Universities will receive a lot of information: predicted grades, GCSE scores, and, if applicable, admissions test scores and some other elements, such as submitted work or an interview. Universities 'use' the UCAS reference in different ways, but it is understood that the UCAS reference no longer plays the significant part in the selection process that it once did.

Who writes the UCAS reference?

A UCAS reference can be written by a teacher, Form Tutor, Careers Adviser or Headteacher. Teachers typically draft comments based on the academic ability and potential of their students. The named referee may be the Headteacher, Head of Sixth Form or Head of Careers.

The writing process will vary across schools and colleges. The UCAS referee is the 'named person', as the referee, but they are seldom the product of one person, particularly in schools and colleges with large cohorts. Unlike most other documents produced by a school, the UCAS reference is collectively drafted and written by multiple authors. References typically take time to write and follow a well-established process:

- Teachers typically draft comments.
- A Form Tutor, UCAS mentor or member of a Sixth Form team collates the information.
- The Head of Careers, Head of Sixth Form or Headteacher finalises the document and uploads it to UCAS.
- The named UCAS referee might do a final check or proofread for quality control, accuracy and parity with other references.

Processing UCAS applications

Over the years, we have developed a system with a 'UCAS final check meeting' for each Year 13 student from September when the student meets with an Adviser to do final checks before their application is sent to UCAS. In this meeting, you could cover the following:

- Check that the student meets the entry requirements at all five of their choices.
- Check that they have one or two Insurance options included in their five choices.
- Show them their predicted grades.
- Read their reference aloud.
- (If applicable) check that they have given their permission for information to be included about any extenuating circumstances in Section 2 of their UCAS reference.

For schools that have subscribed, Unifrog can be used to manage all stages of the reference writing process.

> **QUESTIONS TO CONSIDER**
> - What is this student good at? What do they enjoy doing?
> - Consider their transition from school to university. What are they doing now to develop the skills, habits and routines that will help them make the most of the student experience once there?

Understanding the three sections of the UCAS reference

UCAS reference reforms were introduced for applicants for the 2024 entry onwards. It was reformed from one blank section to three structured sections. The reference has a 4,000-character limit across all three sections. The first section is generic (the same for all students in your school), and the second section is 'optional' and may be left blank. The third section is recommended by the most competitive universities, including the University of Cambridge, the University of Oxford, Durham University and the University of Bath, to name a few. This reform had good intentions, but the 'new-style' reference from one long blank space to three smaller sections has raised questions for schools to address.

Each section requires careful consideration, and UCAS offers guidance on what to include, which we explore further below:

1. Section 1: generic information about your school or college context;
2. Section 2: (optional) information about the impact on education of any extenuating circumstances;
3. Section 3: other information about suitability for the course, based on factual evidence-based statements.

7| Writing University References

UCAS guidance on reference writing:

https://www.ucas.com/advisers/help-and-training/guides-resources-and-training/writing-references/ucas-registered-centre-linked-applications-undergraduate-references

UCAS reference section 1

This section of the reference is the same for each student. It contains information that helps universities understand the context of your school or college. UCAS has plenty of guidance on the sorts of information you could include, with examples of statements. Section 1 is not personalised and is relevant for the whole cohort: type of school, school selection policy, school funding, school performance, qualifications on offer, policy on predictions or any circumstances that have affected the whole cohort. If applicable, you should include any information about serious disruption to the educational provision at your school or college.

The University of Cambridge recommends a maximum of 1,000 characters for this section. Given that the total word count for the whole reference is 4,000 characters, it is advisable to limit the length of your statement to leave space for the other sections, which are personal and specific to the student. You will need to draft, update and reach consensus with your senior colleagues on a suitable Section 1 statement for your educational setting.

What to consider:

- how you will liaise with colleagues to agree on your statement;
- update your statement for each application cycle, as appropriate, to reflect any changes;
- the character count/length of your statement.

UCAS reference section 2

Section 2 is optional. For the majority of students, this section can be left blank by ticking the box to confirm there is no information to enter. However, if relevant, it should be personalised to the student, to include any extenuating circumstances that have affected their education or achievement.

The University of Cambridge recommends a maximum of 500 characters for this section and suggests that if more detail is needed (to be submitted separately), it is appropriate to add this comment in Section 2: 'There is additional information on this applicant we intend to submit.'

Each university has a policy on extenuating circumstances and various forms to fill out. This is important information in terms of making a decision about the application, so the university can consider the student's achievement in context. It may also alert the university to the support that would need to be in place if the student gained admission.

For students who have mitigating circumstances and would like the details to be shared with universities, it is essential to have systems and policies in place. Over the years, we have developed a process with multiple checks: asking students, parents and checking with Form Tutors or Heads of Year. It is important that this information is factual and accurate. It is also likely to be sensitive or possibly confidential information, and it is necessary to gain permission from the student to include this information. Furthermore, you should communicate to students and parents what is and what is not appropriate to include in Section 2 based on UCAS and specific university guidance. In essence, Section 2 should include (if applicable) mitigating circumstances that have disrupted a student's education and achievement.

UCAS offers examples of statements for Section 2: https://www.ucas.com/file/705841/download?token=-OUGsneb

https://www.ucas.com/advisers/help-and-training/guides-resources-and-training/writing-references/ucas-registered-centre-linked-applications-undergraduate-references#reference-guidance

University of Cambridge guidance and examples: https://www.undergraduate.study.cam.ac.uk/apply/how/disrupted-studies

What to consider:

- Are there any extenuating circumstances that affected a student's performance at GCSE or equivalent?
- Are there any extenuating circumstances that might affect a student's performance in their coursework, Year 12 exams or Year 13 final exams?
- Have these circumstances already been considered by the examination boards or awarding organisations for the qualifications taken?

Suggestions:

- Ask students if they would like to have any information included in Box 2.
- Ask Form Tutors to check.
- Ask parents if there is any new information or update.
- Is there additional information that can be sent via a form?

7| Writing University References

Extenuating circumstances letters and forms

These are circumstances that have had an adverse effect on a student's education. This is a notoriously complicated area, given that each university has its own policy, timeframe and bespoke form to complete. As we have discussed, UCAS reference Section 2 can contain the relevant information. However, students might also need to be involved in completing extenuating circumstances forms for universities– which is in addition to their UCAS application. Furthermore, students can contact universities if there is an update after their UCAS application has been sent.

Scenario

You write a letter to Year 12 parents in June with your policy on UCAS references and predicted grades. You mention the following information in your letter: UCAS allows a section in the reference to share any extenuating circumstances that have affected a student's education or achievement. The school is likely to know this information already, but you could invite parents to contact you if there is anything new to report that would be in line with UCAS guidance and fit with similar examples set out by UCAS.

The parent contacts you to explain that they don't want any comments added in Section 2. However, the student has already asked their Form Tutor for Section 2 of the reference to contain information about the impact of their diagnosis of anorexia on their GCSE performance and results. How do you respond to the student and parent?

Suggestions

This is problematic if a parent does not want these comments added, but the student is fine with it. A phone call might be suitable. Try to listen and understand why the parents do not want it acknowledged. Explain that this should not be to the disadvantage of the student; it will allow the universities to appreciate why their lower-than-expected performance at GCSE doesn't match their excellent predicted grades in Year 12. The purpose of Section 2 of the UCAS reference is to allow universities to understand why there is an unusual trajectory. Explain that it might support the applicant, as it will allow the university to better understand their daughter's academic progress.

> **QUESTIONS TO CONSIDER**
>
> - Bristol, Cambridge, Durham University, the University of Exeter, King's College London (KCL) and LSE, among others, have their own extenuating circumstances forms. There are variations in when and who can complete the form. How will you communicate this information to students?

Useful links

- UCAS https://www.ucas.com/advisers/help-and-training/guides-resources-and-training/writing-references/ucas-registered-centre-linked-applications-undergraduate-references
- UCAS sample references and advice https://www.ucas.com/file/705841/download?token=-OUGsneb
- https://www.ucas.com/advisers/writing-references/changes-undergraduate-references-2024-entry
- Universities also publish their own guidance on the new format, which further elaborates on the UCAS requirements. For example:
    - Cambridge University https://www.undergraduate.study.cam.ac.uk/find-out-more/teachers-and-parents/school-college-reference
    - Durham University https://www.durham.ac.uk/study/undergraduate/how-to-apply/guidance-for-teachers-and-advisors/ucas-reference
    - University of Bath https://www.bath.ac.uk/publications/downloadable-guides-to-help-teachers-with-the-application-process/attachments/focus-on-ucas-reference-writing.pdf
    - University of Oxford https://www.ox.ac.uk/admissions/undergraduate/applying-to-oxford/guide/ucas-application

UCAS reference section 3

Section 3 is for other supportive information that is relevant to the applicant or the course they are applying for. The guidance of UCAS has become more prescriptive in recent years, which has been a

7| Writing University References

welcome change in the sector. Consequently, the reference is getting more specific and uniform to write given that it is based on 'factual' and 'evidence-based' statements. Heads of Department can check the quality of the drafting and encourage teachers to stay on track. Statements should be evidence-based, for example:

- X is one of the best students I have ever taught in terms of his engagement in lessons, enthusiasm and intellectual curiosity.
- X scored in the top 5% of the cohort in her Year 12 Chemistry examination.
- X has performed consistently in the top 10% of the cohort in tests and written assignments since joining the Sixth Form.
- X is the best in his class at analysing and interpreting literary texts.
- X has consistently performed in the top half of a high-ability class this year in all aspects of the subject.
- X was one of only three students in the school to achieve a gold award in the X.
- X came sixth in a recent end-of-topic test, from a strong cohort of 79 high-achieving Biology students.

Factual and evidence-based statements are required to show why the student is a suitable candidate for the course they are applying for. In response to UCAS reference reforms, schools have fine-tuned their guidance to the teachers who are drafting recommendations. Teachers cannot go wrong if they follow the guidance: be specific, be factual and use evidence to support factual statements.

For some subjects, such as Medicine, you will need to showcase a student's personal qualities, transferable skills and attributes, and their experience of volunteering and work experience. Consider the advice of UCAS and medical schools, and how you might use your time and expertise to develop your reference writing for applicants to Medicine, Veterinary Science and Dentistry:

https://www.themedicportal.com/teacher-services/how-to-write-a-teacher-reference/

Drafting factual and evidence-based statements

UCAS advice and the requirements of universities such as Cambridge, and so on, require Section 3 to contain factual, evidence-based statements. This presents a challenge for schools. Factual information related to rankings, specific pieces of work, competitions and so on, are arguably more valuable than vague statements about how a student is 'excellent'. However, any 'ranking statement' raises questions about what criteria are used for ranking and how consistently they are applied across different subjects and academic departments in your school or college.

- Ranking in small subjects is very different from larger cohorts.
- Ranking in 'my class' may not be very meaningful.
- If your evidence-based statements are based mostly on Year 12 exam performance, will this increase student stress levels or put undue pressure on them to perform?
- How does one teacher know if a student is the 'best in the whole cohort' if they only teach 15 students etc.?

It is good practice to be specific, for example, referring to specific pieces of work or evidence of a student's particular skills:

- In her coursework focusing on the rise of Julius Caesar, X showed her ability to read primary sources, digest large amounts of information and write coherently and with original thought.
- X's History essays on medieval monarchs have been consistently assessed as being at A* standard.
- X's recent analysis of the topic of market failure was especially insightful and showed clear evidence of deep understanding and wide research.
- In Physics, X is particularly strong in practical work, designing and conducting experiments with focus and enthusiasm.

Subject teachers can draft statements. They can comment on the student's academic suitability for their chosen degree course, particularly if it relates to their own subject. They may wish to comment on the following:

- ability, progress and potential;
- commitment, motivation and diligence;
- capacity for sustained work;
- intellectual inquisitiveness;
- seriousness of purpose;
- creativity or analytical thinking.

The University of Cambridge advice on reference writing:

https://www.undergraduate.study.cam.ac.uk/find-out-more/teachers-and-parents/school-college-reference#:~:text=You%20don't%20need%20to,been%20requested%20will%20be%20disregarded.

QUESTIONS TO CONSIDER

How will you approach UCAS's requirement for evidence-based factual statements?

How do you record and collate data and evidence for producing these factual statements? How will teachers and staff contribute to this?

Scenario

A student contacts you to say that they don't have space in their personal statement to mention their Duke of Edinburgh Gold Award or their Grade 8 Piano. They ask you to include these achievements in their UCAS reference. What do you say to them?

Suggestions

Given that the UCAS reference is academic, this isn't essential information.

Co-curricular activities, while important for developing skills, are not the main focus of an academic reference. Explain that the UCAS reference should focus on academic matters and suitability for a specific course however you could agree to mention this in section 3 of the reference, if there is space. Alternatively they could try and reduce their word count to make space for this information in section 3 of their personal statement.

References and communicating predicted grades

This reference is not available to students, and it is not visible to them on their UCAS application. They can ask their referee for a copy or contact UCAS, who can share a copy under the Data Protection Act.

There are reasons to share the contents of a UCAS reference with a student: they can obtain it via UCAS due to data protection and, while unlikely, it is possible that they may be asked in an interview to respond to a question about a topic mentioned in the reference. However, this is a matter for school policy to decide, and the downside is that it creates an additional layer of work and consultation with the student, along with the risk that they might ask you to change it. Over the years, we have developed a system where a member of staff reads the UCAS reference aloud to the student. Although time-consuming, this strikes a balance.

Action points to consider

Policy

Schools need a policy on the sharing of UCAS references and predicted grades. The UCAS reference should not become a starting point for discussion, and if a student wants you to significantly change or rewrite the reference, this will not only take time but also compromise the UCAS principles on reference writing. If a student wants to question the contents of their reference, how will you manage this? Will your school or college give students or parents an electronic copy of their UCAS reference? Develop a transparent policy that outlines your approach. Make it very clear that the approach to US university references is entirely different, as they are entirely confidential.

> **Scenario**
>
> A parent contacts you via email to request a copy of their daughter's reference before it is sent to UCAS. You reply to their email, outlining that it will be checked by staff and read out to their daughter before the application is sent to UCAS. They respond with a list of bullet points they would like to be included in the UCAS reference, including quotes about the student written by a professional regarding her performance on a work experience placement. The parent requests that the quotes are included and would like to check the contents of the reference before it is sent.
>
> What do you say?

> **Suggestions**
>
> Your reply should reiterate your school policy. You can thank them for the quotes and suggest that they can be considered and could be included if they are appropriate and if there is space. Explain that the contents of the reference must be at the discretion of the school. The focus of the UCAS reference is their academic achievements, based on factual and evidence-based statements from their teachers and their suitability for the course they are applying for.

The application process: Checking and sending to UCAS

When applicants go through 'pay and send' or 'submit and review', their UCAS application is then ready for the school or college to finalise and send. However, students might assume 'pay and send' means their application has gone to the university, rather than to the school. If they have misunderstood this, it can prevent students from completing this vital step and add an extra layer of worry that could slow the process down. Make sure that students realise that they cannot send their application to UCAS; only the school or college can send the application after the student has completed their part.

Students link their application via a 'buzzword', a code that links a UCAS application to your centre. Pressing 'send to UCAS' on an application is a remarkably easy task, and that's the problem. That's why good advisers introduce a rigorous counselling process to make sure that 'the button of doom' is not pressed before time. Once an application has been sent to UCAS, it cannot be edited or changed in any way by the school or college. Students have a 14-day cooling-off window in which they can make limited changes, such as swapping a course, but schools do not have the luxury of a period of grace.

It is hopefully the conclusion following many hours of excellent teaching and careful advice and guidance, which will result in university offers. The staff involved with UCAS would ideally check all elements of an application before it is sent; however, depending on time constraints, you may need to consider how much can be done. The administrative elements of a UCAS application include, but are not limited to, the following:

- Informing students about the UCAS application process and what happens after they complete their part of the application.
- Setting your internal school/college deadlines in order to meet the external UCAS deadlines in October and January.
- Choosing and communicating the buzzword that links your applicants to your school or college.
- Checking the accuracy of the information on the 'student side' of the application, such as their personal information and GCSE or equivalent results.
- Doing a final proofread or check of the reference.
- Approving and sending the UCAS application to UCAS.

> **QUESTIONS TO CONSIDER**
>
> - What are your internal UCAS deadlines for students and staff?
> - Students self-certify their GCSE or equivalent qualifications on their UCAS application. Consider who will check the accuracy of this part of their application? Will you be able to tick the 'qualifications checked' box for all applicants?
> - Students add a fee code, either international (01), home fees (02) or unknown (99). Who will advise them if they are unsure about their fee code?
> - How will you communicate to students and parents about your school policy on UCAS references, confidentiality and so on?
> - How will you allocate time and resources for processing UCAS applications? Who will be responsible for checking, finalising and sending UCAS applications? Who will press the final 'send to UCAS' button on each application?

Links

UCAS Toolkits as a resource:

https://www.ucas.com/file/825601/download?token=Wy3rQ2NV
https://www.ucas.com/advisers/help-and-training/toolkits/2025-cycle-toolkit
https://www.ucas.com/advisers/help-and-training/guides-resources-and-training/writing-references/ucas-registered-centre-linked-applications-undergraduate-references

References for conservatoires for music, drama and dance and universities outside of UCAS

Typically, two references are needed: a practical reference and an academic reference.

How to write UCAS conservatoires references
https://www.ucas.com/conservatoires/filling-your-conservatoires-application/references-conservatoires

Independent applicants

UCAS has advice for independent applicants who may ask an employer to be their referee, with suggestions for what to include in each of the three sections. It is a variation on their advice for school and college references. Individual applicants applying outside your institution do not link to your centre via the buzzword. Instead, the applicant adds the name of the referee who receives a link to upload the reference.

https://www.ucas.com/advisers/help-and-training/guides-resources-and-training/writing-references/writing-undergraduate-references-independent-applicants

Useful links

UCAS examples: https://www.ucas.com/file/705841/download?token=-OUGsneb
UCAS guidance: https://www.ucas.com/advisers/help-and-training/guides-resources-and-training/writing-references/ucas-registered-centre-linked-applications-undergraduate-references
Cambridge University, Writing a Compelling UCAS Reference – YouTube https://www.youtube.com/watch?v=K_Lv3SOQSHI
UCAS reference reform:
https://www.ucas.com/advisers/help-and-training/guides-resources-and-training/writing-references/ucas-registered-centre-linked-applications-undergraduate-references
UCAS references for Medicine: https://www.themedicportal.com/teacher-services/how-to-write-a-teacher-reference/
UCAS advice on individual needs: https://www.ucas.com/undergraduate/what-and-where-study/what-can-i-do-next/undergraduate-individual-needs

Looking ahead: Key takeaways and questions to consider

- *Staff.* Each of the three sections of the UCAS reference needs careful thought: the whole school/college statement (Section 1), relevant extenuating circumstances (Section 2) and any other relevant evidence-based information (Section 3). How will your school or college manage, process and finalise all three sections of the reference?

- *Students.* Depending on what is appropriate in your school or college context, you will need a policy on communicating to students their predicted grades and the content of the reference. What will your policy be, and how will you share relevant information such as students' predicted grades?

8 | Managing university applications: US and international university focus

In this chapter, we suggest ways you can support students applying to universities outside the UK. The first half of this chapter relates to US universities and the second half to other international destinations. Working with students on their university applications can be some of the most fulfilling and rewarding work you can do in a school. In some ways, you sit outside of the normal school structure; on some days, you may find you are doing some of the work you might expect a Form Tutor or Head of Year to do, such as helping a student with organisation, understanding deadlines or staying on track. On other days, you may be more like a teacher, guiding a student in learning new things and in understanding how to research or engage with topics they have not previously encountered. And sometimes, you will be more like a traditional counsellor. At all times, you are an advocate for the student and their guide through a process that may be familiar to you but which is something your student is probably encountering for the first time.

While supporting students with US university applications is incredibly rewarding, it also requires a distinct set of skills and a knowledge base that often take time to develop. This happens mostly through experience. If you're new to university advising, be reassured that there are many things that you will not know at the beginning but that you will learn as you go along. Don't be afraid of what you don't know; you can and should always be learning in this job. This is one of the things that makes this field so rewarding and interesting.

This chapter will cover:

- the role of staff in supporting students with US university applications;
- the elements of a US university application and what students are required to do;

- understanding some key terms;
- admissions test preparation and practice: how to support students taking standardised tests (ACT, SAT and PSAT);
- processing applications, timeline and processes for US applications;
- allocating your time throughout the year;
- helping students with their research;
- encouraging students to look beyond the university name and 'brand';
- the Fulbright Commission, Sutton Trust and understanding financial aid;
- finding your community, networking, university Admissions Officers and independent consultants;
- understanding international universities beyond the US;
- international university applications: resources;
- a brief overview of some international university destinations;
- understanding the selection process and standardised tests: SAT and ACT.

The role of staff in supporting students with US university applications

The wider staff body supplies the US counsellor with information about a student's academic profile and contributions to the wider school environment in the form of teacher recommendations and, often, draft contributions to the counsellor's reference. Make it as easy as possible for teachers to supply this information and ensure that you take into account other responsibilities they may have such as attendance at parents' evenings and the overall reporting cycle when setting your deadlines for supplying material related to US applications. You should always work with the member of SLT who manages this aspect of your school or college when setting internal deadlines.

Make it easy for your colleagues by:

- Being clear about exactly what you require from them and when. Colleagues generally welcome examples of best practices and the opportunity to discuss references, especially if they are new to the US process. Many universities give examples of best practice on their websites; for instance, MIT's guidance can be found here: https://mitadmissions.org/apply/parents-educators/writingrecs/.
- Explaining why their particular contribution is important and how it is viewed by Admissions Officers.
- Building in flexibility when setting deadlines. For example, giving them a term's notice to complete references will avoid unnecessary stress for you and your teaching colleagues.

- Sharing resources with colleagues well in advance of deadlines. Guidance for all recommendations can be found on the Common Application website: https://www.commonapp.org/counselors-and-recommenders/recommender-guide

The elements of a US university application and what students are required to do

The US application process can be onerous as there are multiple components for students to complete which must each be given due care and attention. The application should be seen as one entity composed of multiple parts that all tie into a compelling narrative about the student which the school documents confirm and support.

Help staff understand the US selection process. Good, even excellent, academic grades are not enough; students applying to competitive US universities should consider what they are offering to a university in a holistic sense, not merely an academic one. US universities are looking for community members and active alumni/ae, not just great mathematicians or excellent historians.

Students must complete the following:

- An application; most colleges and universities accept the Common Application, though students should always check if their target school does. Notable exceptions to this are MIT and the University of California system, which use their own application forms.
- Personal statement (often referred to colloquially as 'the Common App essay').
- Supplementary questions and essays related to individual colleges and universities; some institutions do not require supplements, but the vast majority of highly selective/highly rejective institutions do.
- Any required standardised tests (such as the SAT and ACT). Students submit their scores themselves (either self-reported or officially as required by the universities).

Key comparison

US universities are typically interested in the contribution and impact that a student already has made on their school and college community. In general, US universities want to build a class of community members who will add value and have a positive impact.

However, this focus on a student's character and personal attributes contrasts with UK universities, which have a narrower focus on a student's suitability for a specific degree course. American applications not only focus on a student's aptitude but also on their personal journey: challenges they have faced (large or small), their attitude towards difficulties they have encountered and personal qualities such as resilience, kindness and open-mindedness. Excellent grades, though important, are not the only important factor in US university application decisions. Make sure that staff, students and parents understand this crucial difference between these two university systems.

How staff can inspire and advise students to make a competitive application

The best way you can help your students is by getting to know them and providing them with a safe place to express their hopes, fears and worries about the process. In student-centred college counselling, you are there to challenge but also to support. You are the student's advocate and should always treat them with care and respect. This is one of the unquantifiable parts of the job; one student might need much more support than another, even though they are going through the same process. Unlike academic classes, there is no particular pathway to success, nor is there a set syllabus that needs to be mastered. However, there are distinct elements to the role of the US counsellor: helping students shortlist and choose a range of institutions to apply to and supporting them with the different aspects of the applications, such as essay writing.

Staff dealing directly with US university advising should be offered regular opportunities for CPD; this could be external or internal, but it is important that US advising is seen as a constantly evolving process, which staff need time and resources to keep informed about.

Understanding some key terms

Ivy League

This refers to eight universities in the northeast of the US that compete in a sports' league: Cornell, Harvard, Princeton, Columbia, Yale, Dartmouth, Brown and the University of Pennsylvania. They are also perceived as among the most prestigious and best-resourced US universities, and the term is used by many as a by-word for quality. Many students and parents make the mistake of assuming that these universities are similar in outlook and in their approach to education or that they are objectively better than non-Ivy-League universities. Challenge this thinking whenever you can.

Liberal arts colleges

Liberal Arts Colleges are undergraduate-centred institutions that focus on providing a broad-based education across a wide range of humanities and sciences. They emphasise critical thinking, problem-solving and a well-rounded understanding of the world. Students who do well in small group settings and who value close communities often thrive in Liberal Arts Colleges.

Research universities

Research universities are institutions that prioritise research and scholarship in addition to providing an undergraduate education. They often have large graduate programmes and are home to renowned faculty and excellent facilities.

Little Ivies

Little Ivies are a group of small, private Liberal Arts Colleges that are often compared to the Ivy League in terms of academic rigour and selectivity. Some examples include: Amherst College, Williams College, Swarthmore College, Bowdoin College and Smith College. This term is not formally recognised by the colleges themselves but is a useful way to communicate to students that these institutions are well regarded and offer a rigorous programme of study.

Public Ivies

Public Ivies are a group of highly selective public universities that are often compared to the Ivy League in terms of academic rigour and prestige. Examples include the University of California, Berkeley; the University of Michigan; the University of Virginia; the University of North Carolina, Chapel Hill; and the University of Wisconsin–Madison.

Highly selective/highly rejective

Akil Bello coined the phrase 'highly rejective' back in 2021; rather than using the more positive 'highly selective' (which opens the door to students thinking to themselves, '*Why WOULDN'T I be selected; I'm a high achiever*'), the term 'highly rejective' serves to emphasise just how many excellent candidates some institutions turn down each year. For the Ivies, this can be 96% of the applicant pool. Choose one phrase or the other depending on just how punchy you want to be when speaking to students and parents; students who insist on applying to every Ivy League school regardless of knowing much about them tend to respond better to 'highly rejective' as a term.

Identity

All students have an identity that is particular to them; students may have similar profiles, but they are all individuals with thoughts, feelings and ways of seeing the world that are unique to them. Their university application should, as much as possible, convey a sense of this identity and should align with their values and mission.

Mission

It sounds like a slightly grandiose way to put it, but the application shouldn't be only about the pieces of a student's life but how those pieces come together to reflect a student's 'mission'. Students are often intimidated by this idea, but almost without exception, all students have something that they care about, something that they prioritise above other things. Figuring out what this is is crucial to developing an understanding of each particular student's mission, that is, the thing they care about and that they are likely to further develop when they join a university.

Fit

US universities are academic institutions, first and foremost, but they can vary wildly in how academics and the wider culture present. The University of Chicago is very different from Claremont McKenna College, not just in terms of weather but in approach to nearly every aspect of campus and academic life. Students need to understand the vibe and institutional priorities of the universities they are applying to and be sure that it chimes with their values, needs and wants. Regardless of how 'good' an institution purportedly is, if it isn't the right fit for a particular student, the student will not thrive there.

Demonstrated interest

Some US universities are interested in 'demonstrated interest'. This refers to the admissions team at the US college monitoring how much a student has engaged with them, either online or in person. Other universities do not track demonstrated interest at all. If a student is genuinely interested in a university, it is important to learn as much as possible; students can do this easily by attending online information sessions, signing up for university mailing lists and engaging with a university's social media accounts. Students should want to know as much as they can about an institution before potentially spending four years studying there.

Letters of continued interest (LOCIs)

Students who are unsuccessful in applying in any round of the application cycle but who have not been rejected outright can and should write the university a letter of continued interest detailing any progress they have made academically or in any other sphere mentioned in their original application and reiterating their interest in the university.

LOCIs are particularly useful if a student has been 'waitlisted' after the Regular application cycle. They are an opportunity for a student to state a clear commitment to a university, which could be helpful in securing them a place off the waitlist. Students can send LOCIs to all universities on which they have been placed on the waitlist, but they may wish to state to their top choice university that they will enrol if offered a place, and you may wish to follow up and reiterate this to the relevant Admissions Officer. They should only make this statement to one institution; however, one of the functions of an Admissions Officer is to ensure that the incoming class is full and understanding that a student will definitely attend if offered a place can be a positive point in their favour at some universities.

US university applications

In US schools, students are often encouraged, especially by their parents, to begin thinking about school (university) choices earlier than for UK schools. This is a tension that is inherent in different school systems and not one that is easily reconciled, especially if you do not begin your university application preparation until Year 11 or the Sixth Form. Consider if you can start with an introductory session in Year 11. Be prepared for parents to question why you begin offering support when you do, and consider how you will provide them with the information they require without completely changing your own programme.

- In Year 9, parents with an eye on the US may contact you to discuss which GCSEs will make their child competitive for a 'top' university. Our advice is for students to pursue a core of English, a language, sciences and mathematics and then to take additional GCSEs in subjects they feel genuinely interested in.
- In Year 11, you are likely to face the same questions that occurred before the start of GCSE courses. For US university admission, there is no magic combination of subjects that will ensure entry into top universities. Students aiming for top universities should stretch themselves; universities request information about school context when students apply and are interested in understanding whether the courses a student took in Sixth Form were the most academically challenging within their school context.
- For US university entry, Year 12 focuses on understanding how to create a list of universities that typify 'best fit'. Students should begin (and ideally complete) their application essay (generally the Common Application essay for the majority of US applications) and fill out the relevant application forms (Common Application, Coalition Application or the university's own application).
- In Year 13, students make their applications. Early Application and Early Decision round applications are generally made before 1 November, and Regular round applications around 1 January.

Admissions test preparation and practice: how to support students taking standardised tests (ACT, SAT and PSAT)

Many well-known universities require standardised testing of some sort, though some notable names, such as NYU, have been test-optional for many years now. It is worth checking universities' policies and asking Admissions Officers as to how they use test scores in their admissions processes; for students who struggle with test-taking of this sort, applying to an institution that relies heavily on the test score as a data point may not be the best use of that student's time.

Universities requiring testing will generally accept both the SAT and ACT. Students can take these multiple times and, for some institutions, can 'superscore' their results, that is, combine the highest score for each section across multiple sittings of the test in order to come up with their superscore. Notably, Georgetown requires students to submit scores from all sittings of an exam so that they can understand how many times a student had to take the exam in order to get the highest score possible.

Schools approach standardised test preparation in a variety of ways. Some schools may choose to bring an external provider in to teach students across a number of sessions, anywhere from three to 10 sessions overall. Other schools will give students the basic details of the exams (https://satsuite.collegeboard.org/sat and https://www.act.org/) and encourage them to use the online practice tests provided by the board with additional tuition by a private company or tutor if required. Many companies offer standardised test 'boot camps' during school holidays, which can be helpful for students who struggle with managing their test prep on their own. Many bright and motivated students self-study without using any additional services.

If you work at a school attended by American citizens, you may have parents asking about the PSAT (the Preliminary SAT), which only US citizens are eligible to take. The PSAT allows access to certain scholarships (including the National Merit Scholarship), so it may be worth your student(s) taking it. If you do not have the facility to enable the test to be taken at your school, students can take it at a school they do not attend; however, they will need to contact the school at which they would like to sit the exam well in advance. https://satsuite.collegeboard.org/psat-nmsqt/taking-the-test/international-registrations

Processing applications, timeline and processes for US applications

	Student activities and internal deadlines	Staff activities and internal deadlines	External deadlines
Year 12 Term 1	Students should attend any US university visits happening on campus (these usually take place in September and early October around the time of USA College Day). You may wish to offer these opportunities to your Year 11 cohort as well if appropriate for your setting.	Introduce your programme and explain how the US application process works at your school or college. Consider holding an online or in-person information event for parents to consider the process.	None
Year 12 Term 2	Start whole group meetings in which you explain information relevant to the entire cohort. Run a series of two to three mandatory general information sessions and then ask students to reconfirm their interest. Continue to run mandatory information sessions every week until the end of term. Students should ideally have their first one-to-one meeting with their US Adviser before the end of this term.	Allocate US Advisers to specific students who have confirmed their interest in applying after attending mandatory group meetings.	None

Year 12 Term 3	Students should have at least one further one-to-one meeting with their US Adviser before the end of term. Students should create Common App accounts and link these to whichever sending platform they are using (for example, Bridge-U or Unifrog). Students should request recommendations from two teachers of different subjects early in this term (with references due by the end of this term).	US Advisers should be available to meet with students on a casual basis throughout this term. Office hours help facilitate this. Teaching staff should complete and submit their teacher recommendations to the Head of US Applications for proofreading by the end of this term. If Form Tutors or other members of staff are providing information for the counsellor reference, this material should be submitted by the end of this term ideally.	Some external scholarship nomination deadlines fall at the end of this term (for example, the Morehead-Cain scholarship at the University of North Carolina at Chapel Hill).
Year 13 Term 1	Early Action and Early Decision applications internal deadline should be before half-term. Regular Decision applications internal deadline should be before the end of this term. Students should consider whether they will apply for financial aid at their chosen institutions (if available to students of their nationality).	The school side of applications (transcripts, references and any additional supporting material) should be submitted before the application deadline.	Early Action and Early Decision applications are due (generally around 1 November) Regular Decision applications are due during the holiday break. N.B. University of California and some other state university system applications are due in November.

	Student activities and internal deadlines	Staff activities and internal deadlines	External deadlines
Year 13 Term 2	Submission of any applications with a deadline falling during this term.	Mid-year reports should be submitted in January/February.	Mid-year reports due
Year 13 Term 3	All offers are generally received by 1 April; students should accept one offer only through their university portals and decline all other offers. The deadline for this is generally around 1 May. Students who are waitlisted may wish to submit a LOCI to one or more institutions.	Final reports should be submitted as soon as possible following Results Day.	Final reports due

8| Managing University Applications: US and International University Focus

Allocating your time throughout the year

If you are working within a school that has only a few US and international applications each year, you may find that you are the only person with responsibility for these applications. If you have a larger cohort of students applying to the US, there may be other members of staff with time allocated to helping you. When considering how to divide the work required to manage the school side of US applications, you may want to split the job into two distinct parts: the administrative side and the counselling side.

The amount of time you provide each student for one-to-one meetings and interactions will vary according to your school context, but it is reasonable to budget an average of between 10 and 30 minutes per student per week, with the understanding that at some points in the year, you will be on the '10 minutes' end of the spectrum and at other points you will be at the '30 minutes' end of the spectrum. Demand for individual support tends to be greater in the autumn term, especially for students who require additional support for whatever reason. If your school expects you to advise students and process applications, you will need to further consider how you will use the time and resources available, discussed in Chapter 4.

Develop a set of questions you will ask students in individual meetings. Suggested starting points can be found below. All of your questions should help you get to know the student better. Asking them to expand on their answers and giving them the time and space to do this will not only help you develop a better understanding of and relationship with them, but it will also allow you to advise them appropriately. At all times, you should try to approach advising as a student-centred and, as much as possible, a student-led set of activities. You are there to help guide and support them, not to tell them what to do.

Suggestions for questions

- Tell me about yourself. As in, what has made you the person you are today? This could be various factors such as a geographical location, a group of people like your family or a group of friends, a team you belong to or a hobby you love. What are some of the key things that make you who you are?
- What subjects do you enjoy? Why?
- What makes you interested in studying in America? What do you know about America already?

- Do you have any universities or colleges you are already interested in? Tell me what you know about them.
- What do your parents or guardians think about you studying in America?
- Have you thought about what you would like to write your personal essay about?
- How is school at the moment?
- How is your research going? Have you found any colleges or universities you're excited about? Tell me what you love about them.
- Would you like to apply Early Action or Early Decision?

Helping students with their research

There are resources available to help you and your students, and we strongly encourage you to make use of the help that universities themselves, governmental bodies and outside consultants can provide. The most compelling applications are those in which a student demonstrates a clear understanding of themselves and can make a case for how attending a specific institution will benefit both themselves and that institution.

Students should be encouraged to look beyond the university names that they already know. A good exercise is to ask students to choose one of the following websites (or similar) and to create a long list of 10–15 universities in which they are interested based on fairly standard parameters such as location, size, availability of specific programmes or courses and anything else that is particularly important to the student.

Websites for initial research:

Niche (www.niche.com) gives colleges and universities a 'report card' style grading based on various aspects of university life.

The College Board (https://bigfuture.collegeboard.org) is the organisation that runs the SAT; they also have a university search function that students can use to learn about various institutions.

Colleges That Change Lives (https://ctcl.org) is an organisation that stems from Loren Pope's 1996 book of the same name. This group of institutions is less known by international students; this is an excellent resource to introduce them to colleges they might not discover on their own.

Encourage the student to keep notes, either on paper or electronically. They are often surprised by how easily they forget which university offers something incredible that they just can't imagine missing out on. This part of the process is a good time to remind them that universities are excellent at marketing for the most part. In the photographs on their websites, students will always be smiling, sitting on beautiful green lawns with impressive buildings behind them or laughing with a group of friends. That is the nature of marketing. But emphasise to your students that it is exceptionally important to look beyond 'the name' and beyond the marketing to understand what an institution is really like and what it values. Another practical tip is for students to research into the foundation and history of particular US universities to discover the principles they were founded on.

Individual university websites and their social media are obviously good places to look, but they are also tools for marketing; more interesting is looking beyond that, at press releases put out by the university (what is being highlighted?), at LinkedIn posts (what do these institutions want the professional world to see?) and at university mission statements.

Students do sometimes gravitate to videos made by their near-peers that purport to represent 'the truth' about a specific institution. Advise your students to treat these with caution. In the case of YouTube or TikTok video reviews, remind them that people who make this content are generally on one extreme or the other; either very, very happy and satisfied or very, very unhappy and dissatisfied. This content is most useful to lead students to do further research about particular aspects of that university or location that might not be a good fit for them. For example, if you have a student with particular academic support needs, or who will be a minority student on campus, this content may be a way for them to get a more in-depth understanding of what it might be like for them on that campus, which they can then follow up on either through contact with the Admissions Office or in a conversation with you.

Encouraging students to look beyond the university name and 'brand'

Students in the UK tend to gravitate towards 'name' universities that they have heard of when making their US university lists; while this might be frustrating if you are trying to encourage students to focus on universities that fit them, there is some logic behind this approach on the part of students. With well-ranked universities on their doorstep (and access to student finance), for some students, there is little reason to leave the UK unless the university they attend is substantially 'better' than one they could go to in the UK.

Parents can also be focused on brand when discussing university applications. Gaining a university offer is not like winning a prize; it is an invitation to join an educational institution and the start of a new chapter. This is worth reiterating as much as possible throughout the process.

For students who are looking for an alternative style of teaching from that found at the majority of UK universities but who are not able or willing to relocate to America, a number of US universities or US-style universities also operate outside the US, for example, The American University of Paris (France), Franklin University (Switzerland), John Cabot (Italy) and Richmond University (England). Some UK universities, such as UEA, also offer study abroad opportunities in the US.

The Fulbright Commission, Sutton Trust and understanding financial aid

The US-UK Fulbright Commission is a non-profit organisation dedicated to promoting cultural understanding between the US and the UK primarily through academic grants. It was established in 1948 and is based in London. The Fulbright Commission's biggest event each year is USA College Day, which generally happens at the end of September each year. They also offer regular training to teachers throughout the year.

The Sutton Trust is a UK-based charity that has social mobility as one of its primary focuses. Through various initiatives, the Trust helps young people from less advantaged backgrounds with Careers guidance and university access, including to top universities in the US. They run a series of summer schools that allow students to visit and learn at leading universities in the UK and the US free of charge. These programmes are only available to students who have always studied at a state school.

Understanding merit- and needs-based financial aid

One of the best sources of information about financial aid available to non-US citizens is compiled each year by Jennie Kent and Jeff Levy of Big J Educational Consulting. The resources page of their website is full of easily digestible data, which you can and should use in conversations with your students and parents. https://www.bigjeducationalconsulting.com/resources

Merit-based competitive scholarship programmes in the US include (but are not limited to):

- The Morehead-Cain (UNC-Chapel Hill);
- The Belk (Davidson);
- The Jefferson (University of Virginia);
- The Robertson (UNC and Duke).

These scholarships are highly prestigious and competitive, offering significant financial aid and opportunities for academic and personal growth. All four scholarships prioritise academic achievement and emphasise leadership as a key factor in choosing scholarship recipients. Each scholarship also values a commitment to service and community engagement.

You should advise students to check whether an institution takes into consideration whether they are asking for financial aid at the point of application; some universities take these requests into consideration when making admissions decisions and will deny students they do not believe they can support with a competitive financial aid package offer. Often a student cannot apply for aid after admission, so if a student needs financial aid, or may need it at any point in their undergraduate career, they should apply for it. Parents with questions about potential financial aid or financial aid packages should liaise directly with institutions' financial aid offices who will be better placed to help them than you are.

Recruited athletes and sports scholarships

If you have students seeking athletic recruitment, advise students and families to be cautious about using agents that promise recruitment at specific universities or 'sports scholarships'. Note that the timeline for athletic recruitment tends to run approximately one year earlier than students making standard applications; so, for instance, a student athlete might be approached by an athletic recruiter or coach from a university during Year 10 or Year 11, work on their applications in Year 12 and submit as soon as the admissions cycle opens in Year 13. They may also be asked to submit materials for a 'pre-read' (generally in the spring of Year 12); if they are asked to do this, you will need to ensure you have a transcript and references ready for them early.

Finding your community, networking, university Admissions Officers and independent consultants

Online communities and groups:

There are numerous online communities (generally housed on Facebook, LinkedIn and the Times Higher Education Counsellor website) that are full of other Advisers and counsellors, who are often very happy to give advice and to commiserate.

In-person events:

In the UK, there are a number of consultants and companies that provide support for students, but very few of these provide support to teachers who are doing this job. UES Education is one of the primary companies that provide support for teachers through their school services and through their in-person conference that happens annually and other smaller events throughout the year.

You may also like to join a professional body such as IACAC (the International Association for College Admissions Counseling), which also runs international conferences on US admissions that happen yearly in different locations around the world. US universities often run counsellor fly-ins either timed around major conferences, such as the IACAC annual conference, or at other times of the year. In some cases, the full cost of travel and accommodation is covered by the university. As you make connections with university Admissions Officers, it never hurts to ask if they run counsellor fly-ins and whether you could join the list for future events.

Admissions Officers

Unlike many UK universities, US universities employ staff whose sole job it is to deal with admissions for their institutions. These Admissions Officers have responsibility not only for reviewing applications but also for managing their particular territories, which often includes travelling to schools and building relationships with students and college counsellors. Admissions Officers tend to be outgoing, friendly people (they wouldn't be in a people-centred business if they weren't); building a respectful and friendly relationship with Admissions Officers is mutually beneficial. You want admissions teams to understand your students and your context.

As you build your programme, pay attention to what types of institutions are a 'good fit' for your students as well as where your students actually apply. Don't be afraid to reach out to the Admissions Officer who handles your region at any university you would like your students to engage with and ask them if they are likely to be travelling to your area and if they can visit. Many admissions representatives travel at the start of the autumn term around the Fulbright Commission's USA College Day, which is usually held at the end of September each year. Requesting a visit is not seen as pushy or rude.

Scenario

Student B is an international student whose parents attended university. They have high expectations of B and expect them to go to a 'well-ranked' university. They would like B to go to 'the best' university possible.

Suggestions

- Try and ascertain from the student where they would like to go. Be aware of and sympathetic to the pressures that the student might be under from the parents.
- Unpick what 'the best' is. For some parents, this could be based on rankings such as the *Times Higher Education* or *QS* rankings or different ideas about what constitutes 'the best' for their daughter or son.
- Ensure that you write up the notes and outcome of any decisions you have with the student and parents and distribute them to all relevant stakeholders (student, parents, relevant Form Tutor or Head of Year).

Scenario

A Year 13 student who has just left your school is looking forward to taking up their offer at a US university. They receive their exam results in August and have fallen significantly short of their predicted grades. What should happen next?

Suggestions

Universities expect students to meet the predictions sent to them throughout the application process (the transcript, mid-year report and final report). This puts an onus on both you as a school to issue accurate predictions and on the student to meet these predictions. Some students perceive US offers as being unconditional, but this is not the case, and you should make this clear to students and parents throughout the process.

However, students do sometimes miss their predictions; you should provide guidance prior to exam Results Day as to actions students need to take if they find themselves in this situation. You should also be prepared to assist students on exam Results Day or ensure that another briefed member of staff is able to support students and communicate with Admissions Officers at relevant institutions.

As soon as results are released to your school, but before students can access them, note who has missed their predictions and by how much. Keep a list of misses that are significant; a general rule of thumb might be that universities need to be contacted if a student has dropped more than 3 points for IB and 2 or more grades for A level students. Once results are released, monitor whether these students or their parents have been in contact; if the student has missed their predictions by a significant amount, you may consider proactively emailing the student and contacting them to get in touch with the universities. Copy the student's parent into your correspondence unless there's a reason not to, as students might appreciate some clarity and reassurance if they are frightened about having an offer rescinded. They need your patience and support regardless of why they missed their predicted grades.

Do not feel that you need to email Admissions Officers in order to sort things out on behalf of students; the students themselves must email the universities and explain the issue and whether there were any mitigating factors that led to the underperformance.

Obviously, if there are no mitigating circumstances, you need to be careful of what you say in your correspondence to the university. Do not make excuses for students where there are none; universities rely on you as the representative of your institution to be honest. Universities get to know individual schools, and they can track the accuracy of predictions. You have a responsibility not only to your current students but to all the students who will apply from your school in the future.

A word about Independent Educational Consultants (IECs)

An IEC is a private counsellor who is paid for by parents. These consultants come from many backgrounds; they may have been a school-based counsellor or a member of a university admissions team. Anyone can set themselves up as an IEC, and some are more ethical and knowledgeable than others. You are not responsible for making recommendations about specific consultants, but you could suggest that students work with IECs who have worked with people they know personally; if no one at your school has applied to the US before, suggest that students ask their potential consultant for the contact details of a student who worked with them in the previous admissions cycle. Reputable consultants are likely to belong to organisations such as IACAC, the Council of International Schools or the IECs Association.

8| Managing University Applications: US and International University Focus

Useful links

Independent educational consultants provide online resources and in-person events for students, teachers and parents:

- The University Guys https://www.theuniversityguys.com
- UES https://www.ueseducation.com
- Vela Education https://velaeducation.com/

The Fulbright Commission and EducationUSA (part of the US Department of State) offers advice to students, parents and schools on all aspects of the US application process https://fulbright.org.uk.

Understanding international universities beyond the US

If you are working with a group of students who are interested in applying to universities in the US, they may also be willing to look at other university systems worldwide. This can be a very complex undertaking, as the university application system in different countries can vary considerably, sometimes even from university to university.

Where in the world your cohort tends to apply will somewhat depend on the specifics of that group of students; if you are working with students who need financial support in order to take up their university places, you may be looking at a very specific group of US universities and, perhaps, merit-based aid available at Canadian universities. Alternatively, if your students are not limited by cost, you may find that they apply to an enormous range of courses all over the world in the pursuit of 'the best' offer they can get. If your students tend to have multiple passports, you'll often find that they apply to the US, the UK and their 'home' system; if they speak multiple languages, they will be able to access courses taught in English and in their native, second or even third language. Keep all of this in mind as you plan the support you will offer them.

When you first meet a cohort of students, ascertain what their likely pathways will be. A brief survey early in Year 12 can be an enormous help in understanding where your students are interested in applying; you can then ensure that you are armed with the information you will need to guide and support them. Keep records so that you can track their applications outside of UCAS.

International university applications: A brief guide

International university counselling is an expertise and a specialism in its own right, and students' interest in applying to universities outside the

UK has grown considerably in the past 20 years. There are international options for students to consider; for example, Forward College offers a degree programme (accredited by the University of London) taught across Lisbon, Paris and Berlin, allowing students to spend a year in each of these three cities. There are specialist Swiss hotel schools for students who want to specialise in hospitality.

Two key aspects of studying in Europe have fundamentally changed in the past 5–10 years:

- The United Kingdom has left the European Union, and with that, British students have lost the reduced fee status they previously were able to access at many EU institutions. This has made European destinations a less attractive prospect financially for British students.
- International universities, particularly European universities, have increased the number of courses that they offer that are taught in English.

These two facts have changed the way UK-based students perceive and approach European applications.

International university application requirements vary considerably from country to country and can change with little warning. Below, we detail the main university systems students attending a UK or British-pattern school outside the UK may apply to. You and your students are strongly advised to check the websites listed below (many of which are government-run sources of information) as well as looking at the webpages of each university a student is interested in, as requirements can vary from university to university even within the same country.

International university applications: Resources

Your role is to support students with their university applications and point them in the right direction for their research. If you have recently started advising students on international destinations, take time to understand the requirements of the university systems likely to be of interest to your students. Ensure you understand if there are any subject requirements that students must meet (for example, Germany and Switzerland have specific subject requirements that students should be aware of, preferably in advance of choosing their A level or IB subjects; https://www.swissuniversities.ch/en/topics/studying/admission-to-universities/ and https://www.daad.de/en/studying-in-germany/requirements/gce/).

Admissions representatives from each international system are also a very useful point of call for particular questions you may have. They

8| Managing University Applications: US and International University Focus

often travel and are happy to visit schools either in person or as part of online information sessions.

The University Guys have a series of very useful information guides available on their website for universities worldwide (https://www.theuniversityguys.com/knowledge/guides/), which are an excellent starting point for understanding the nuances of each application system. This information is relevant for parents, students and staff.

Study Options has a wealth of excellent information on their website and also runs fairs with university reps from Australia and New Zealand most years: https://studyoptions.com.

> **PRACTICAL TOOLS AND TIPS**
>
> **Unifrog**
>
> If your school subscribes to Unifrog, make sure that students and parents are aware of the huge number of resources available on the platform that give detailed information about applying to universities worldwide.
>
> **Counsellor fly-ins**
>
> Many international universities offer counsellor fly-ins, which are tours of universities or a group of universities that help counsellors understand those universities better. They are often arranged by the universities themselves, by consortia of universities or sometimes by governmental organisations. Contact your regional representative if you are interested in attending a fly-in.

Spotlight on Canadian universities: A North American alternative

International applications to Canadian universities are typically less onerous for schools to manage than US applications. For example, Canadian university applications typically don't require school references, making the applications more straightforward for a school to manage. Unlike US universities, Canadian universities don't require standardised tests, which students might find appealing. Canadian universities might suit students who are less decided on course choice given that they apply to a faculty (not a course) such as 'Arts', 'Science' or 'Engineering'. Renowned for balancing academic study with work placements, Canadian degree courses typically integrate 'co-op' programmes, work experience and internships.

Within the University of British Columbia there are two campuses, the main campus in Vancouver and the satellite campus, Okanagan located in

Kelowna and each campus has different requirements and specialisms. Similarly, McGill has two campuses, one in Montreal and the Macdonald campus in Sainte-Anne-de-Bellevue. The University of Toronto has three campuses: the main St George campus, Scarborough and Mississauga.

Canadian universities are well known for their 'co-op' programmes and opportunities for work placements. The application process is relatively straightforward: students declare their predicted grades and submit additional materials as required, such as videos for some courses.

For example, for the University of Toronto, students can select up to three courses but only one course 'per division'. Levels of competition vary between courses, and they need to meet the subject-specific prerequisites. Applicants apply in Year 13, and from November to January, with decisions released from January until May. Schools can nominate exceptional students who they consider suitable for the University of Toronto full-ride Pearson Scholarship. Students need a provisional attestation letter (PAL) to apply for a study permit in Canada.

PRACTICAL TOOLS AND TIPS

One of the pitfalls of international university admissions is navigating the choices available. Students can struggle to research, make sense of and identify universities that are a 'good fit' for them or which institutions and courses might be a suitable Plan B option. Reverse admissions offer something of a solution, whereby universities across the world select students directly.

In contrast to direct admissions, where students select and apply to the university, with reverse admissions the university finds the student, either by inviting them to apply (such as via METO) or making them a direct offer (via Concourse).

For example, students can register for free with METO to find out if international universities would like to receive an application from them: https://meto-intl.org. Concourse, which facilitates the making of university offers to students, is free to CIS accredited schools, but individual students can register for a small fee: https://discover.concourseglobal.net/student/start. Consider if you think this approach might benefit your students.

At the time of writing, there are currently only a few UK universities using a reverse admissions process. Information on reverse admissions can be found here: https://www.timeshigher education.com/counsellor/admissions-processes-and-funding/what-are-reverse-admissions-and-why-do-they-matter; https://www.ueseducation.com/ues-education-blog/reverse-admissions-with-concoursemode_comment

Dual/triple degree programmes

Students who are interested in having a university experience in multiple countries and multiple institutions should consider dual/triple degree programmes. For example:

- University of St Andrews in Scotland and William and Mary in the US offer a Joint degree programme where students spend two years studying at each institution.
- University College London and Sciences Po in France offer a Dual Degree Programme in European Social and Political Sciences; Sciences Po also offers joint programmes with the University of California at Berkeley and Columbia in New York, among other international partners.
- Ecole Polytechnique in France and Columbia in the US offer a Dual Degree Engineering programme with a three-year bachelor's degree in France followed by a two-year master's programme in the US.
- The University of Southern California, Bocconi in Milan and the Hong Kong University of Science and Technology offer the World Bachelor in Business, a four-year programme.
- University College London and Hong Kong University offer a dual Bachelor of Laws, with two years in each country.

A brief overview of some international university destinations

Many international university systems offer courses taught in English; if you have students who are willing to look outside the UK, it is worth exploring these options with them. The application systems for each country vary considerably, and it is worth taking the time to engage with university representatives and university information sessions.

Australia and New Zealand

- **Universities:** University of Melbourne, University of Sydney, University of Western Australia, Edith Cowen, University of Queensland and University of Otago.
- **Other Information:** Non-Australian and New Zealand citizens can apply for free through Study Options, a UK-based organisation that works in conjunction with the governments of Australia and New Zealand.
    - Study in Australia: https://www.studyaustralia.gov.au/
    - Study in New Zealand: https://www.studywithnewzealand.govt.nz/en
    - Study Options: https://studyoptions.com/

Canada

- **Universities:** University of Toronto, McGill University and University of British Columbia.
- **Other Information:** Students with French citizenship can study at a reduced rate in Quebec.
    - Study in Canada: https://www.canada.ca/en/immigration-refugees-citizenship/services/study-canada.html
    - Canadian Universities: https://univcan.ca/

China

- **Universities:** Peking University, Tsinghua University, Fudan University and Shanghai Jiao Tong University
    - Study in China: https://studyinchina.edu.cn/
    - Chinese Universities: http://np.china-embassy.gov.cn/eng/StudyinChina/dxwz/

France

- **Universities:** Sciences Po joint programmes (see previous pages); The American University of Paris.
- Campus France: https://www.campusfrance.org/fr
    - https://www.sciencespo.fr/college/en/academics/dual-bachelor-degrees/

Germany

- **Universities:** Humboldt University of Berlin, Ludwig Maximilian University of Munich, Technical University of Munich, Heidelberg University and Bard Berlin.
- Study in Germany: https://www.study-in-germany.de/en/
    - German Academic Exchange Service (DAAD): https://www.daad.de/en/

Hong Kong

- **Universities:** The University of Hong Kong, Hong Kong University of Science and Technology, and Chinese University of Hong Kong.
    - Study in Hong Kong: https://studyinhongkong.edu.hk/

Ireland

- **Universities**: Over 40 HEIs with most in Dublin, including TCD and UCD.

8| Managing University Applications: US and International University Focus

- UK, EU, EEA and Swiss citizens can apply to Irish Higher Education institutions via the Central Applications Office (CAO) https://www.cao.ie. This website contains comprehensive information about courses, HEI's, the application process, deadlines, offer rounds and links to useful resources. Citizens of countries other than those listed above apply directly to the university and should check carefully the requirements for admission well in advance of their intended application.

Italy

- **Universities:** Bocconi, The American University of Rome and John Cabot University.
- Study in Italy: https://studyinitaly.esteri.it/
  - Italian Universities: https://www.unibo.it/en

Japan

- **Universities:** The University of Tokyo, Kyoto University, Osaka University and Tokyo Institute of Technology.
- Study in Japan: https://www.studyinjapan.go.jp/en/
  - Japanese Universities: https://www.aatj.org/students/study abroad/college-university-programs/

Netherlands

- **Universities:** University of Amsterdam, Leiden University, Erasmus University Rotterdam and Maastricht University.
- Study in Holland: https://www.studyinnl.org/

Norway, Sweden and Denmark

- **Universities:** University of Oslo, Lund University, University of Copenhagen and University of Gothenburg.
  - Study in Norway. https://www.studyinnorway.no/
  - Study in Sweden: https://studyinsweden.se/
  - Study in Denmark: https://studyindenmark.dk/

Spain

- **Universities:** IE, St. Louis University
  - Study in Spain: https://www.study.eu/country/spain

Switzerland

- **Universities:** ETH Zurich, University of Zurich, University of Geneva and University of Lausanne.
- Swiss Universities: https://www.swissuniversities.ch/en/
  - Study in Switzerland: https://www.studyinswitzerland.plus/

> **Scenario**
>
> Student A is planning to apply to multiple application systems, including the US, the UK, Europe and Canada. The student's parents have high expectations of A and expect them to go to a 'well-ranked' university. They would like A to stay in the UK for university but know people whose children have gone to American universities. They will allow A to go to the US if A can get into a 'better' university than they can in the UK.

> **Suggestions**
>
> - What do the parents perceive as the definition of 'better'?
> - What does the student perceive as the definition of 'better'?
> - Would the parents consider universities outside of the US or UK?
> - If financial aid is required, are the student and parents aware of the limitations this may place on their options and chances of acceptance?
>
> If possible, often a conversation with the parents and the student, as well as a Form Tutor, Head of Year or other colleague, can help tease out any mixed messages or misperceptions that the parent and student may have and can also clarify for both what the other is thinking. In this scenario you are likely to be both providing information but also potentially acting as a mediator between the student and their parents.
>
> As with all students applying to multiple application systems while also juggling A levels or the IB, everyone needs to be aware of the time commitment intrinsic in applying to the US as well as to the UK, especially if the student is applying to a UK university that requires admissions tests and interviews. The student may need a support plan in place in order to help them manage the workload.

Looking ahead: Key takeaways and questions to consider

- *Staff.* US and international counselling is a specialist area of expertise, and staff need adequate time and support to complete the required work as well as to engage with **Continuing Professional Development.** How will you staff and resource this?

- *Students.* **US university applications require students to spend significant time away from their academic studies.** How might you increase students' awareness of US and other international universities and help them prepare and maximise their chances of making successful applications?

- *Parents.* **International university applications vary across countries.** How might you communicate reliable and relevant information to parents about universities outside the UK?

9 | Writing university references and supporting application essays: US focus

US university applications are 'a marathon, not a sprint', which can make it tricky for both students and Advisers. Because the process can take anywhere between a term to several years to complete, carefully managing your students' application timeline is crucial. The US university application process is a strenuous and time-consuming application process, perhaps second only to preparing a competitive UCAS Medicine application. The process requires students to reflect on who they are, what they value and what contributions they hope to make on their future campuses; it is the polar opposite of the majority of other university systems where academic achievement determines whether a student will be given an offer. Despite how challenging it can be, for many students, the US application process can be extremely rewarding if they see it as an opportunity for personal growth and development.

This chapter will cover:

- the key elements of a US application;
- school documents: school profile, transcript, mid-year report and final report;
- teacher references to support US university applicants;
- the counsellor reference to support US university applicants;
- uploading and sending documents to US universities: Common App, Bridge-U and Unifrog;
- Early and Regular round applications;
- the US application essay and supplemental essays: helping students manage the writing process.

The key elements of a US application

The documents required by colleges and universities in the States are numerous. Each student's US application is composed of two distinct parts: a 'school side' and a 'student side'. School documents fall into two categories themselves: administrative documents such as transcripts, mid-year reports and final reports, and then documents that require personalised input such as references.

School documents:

- school profile;
- transcript;
- mid-year report;
- final report;
- teacher recommendations;
- counsellor reference.

Student documents:

- **The application** which may include a personal essay and supplementary essays.
    - Most US applications are submitted through the Common Application, though there are notable exceptions to this: MIT and the University of California system have their own application forms/portals that students must apply through. Whatever the portal, the student is likely to need a personal essay and potentially supplementary essays detailing their suitability for the specific institution to which they are applying.
    - While it is important that you have an understanding of which universities require which application systems, the onus should always be on the student to ensure that they have understood the requirements of each application they are making. Encourage/require them to check these requirements themselves and make it clear that this is their responsibility, not yours.
- **Additional portfolios or writing samples.** This will be dependent on whether the student is applying for specific courses, such as performance courses. Some universities also ask students to submit writing samples. All universities asking for additional material give detailed instructions on their websites regarding how to fulfil these requirements.

School documents: School profile, transcript, mid-year report and final report

School profile

Universities rely on information provided in the school profile in order to understand each applicant from your school within your school context.

Transcript

A record of a student's grades over the four years prior to their application.

Transcripts should list each course a student has taken during their four years of high school (UK Years 10–13). Students must include examination results for every exam taken, even if they later resat the exam.

Mid-year report

Submitted in late January or early February, this is a document that reports on a student's academic progress. This document is submitted by the school, not the student. In schools using predicted grades, this report is often a reiteration of the previous set of predictions unless there is documented cause for concern. Student predictions should only be changed in line with school policy and with the knowledge of the member of SLT with responsibility for academics. Some universities may ask for a First Quarter Grade Report in November for students who have applied in the Early round; this aligns with the US school calendar and is intended to check whether students are maintaining their academic level during their final year of school. If you are working within a British-pattern or IBDP school, it is acceptable to submit the transcript you have already sent for the student containing their predicted grades but relabelled as a First Quarter Grade Report.

Final report

Submitted as soon after exam Results Day as possible (July for the IBDP, August for A levels etc.), this is a document that details the final results a student has received. Students may also need to arrange for official results to be sent by the boards or the IBO. The template for this document can be exactly the same as the Transcript and Mid Year Report but with the final grades added and the heading changed. This will save you time when you may need to issue a number of transcripts in a very short window of time.

Teacher references to support US university applicants

The College Board describes the role of the teacher recommendation as an *'honest appraisal . . . of a student's academic performance and intellectual promise'*. Admissions Officers are looking to understand what the student is like in the classroom and what sort of student they will be when they appear on a US college campus.

Students generally require two teacher references (referred to interchangeably as 'recommendations'). Although some colleges will accept only one or even no recommendations, students should always ask two teachers to write on their behalf so that they have the required number should they decide late in the application cycle to apply to universities that require more than one. Be careful that students are clear about what kind of references are required by individual institutions; for example, MIT notably requires a humanities and a STEM reference. **Students should never be shown academic references for US applications, as they are confidential.**

Teachers typically take reference writing extremely seriously; they want to do a good job for their students, but they may not have experience writing US-style references. Ensure that they have been given good guidance and some examples if possible. Teachers in British schools are sometimes reluctant to use too many superlatives, seeing this as 'braggy' or exaggerated. Remind the teachers who their audience is: Admissions Officers want to hear the best (true) things a teacher can tell them about the student; they are keen to understand what kind of learner and member of the community the student is and the teacher is the best person who can give them that understanding. Statistics about a student's academic capabilities in relation to the rest of the cohort are helpful to include, as are detailed anecdotes about students.

Questions to address in a teacher recommendation:

- What evidence have you seen that this student will be an active member of the university's academic community?
- How might this student contribute to the university community in other ways?
- What makes this student special in your view?
- Can you think of a time when this student really excelled?
- Are they a leader or more of a supporter during class discussions?
- Are there any specific pieces of work they've completed that have set them apart from the others?
- What are they like during your lessons?

US teacher references: key points to keep in mind.

- The entire reference should not exceed a page.
- The reference should be about the student, not what is covered in the course.
- Teachers should highlight the student's strengths. The student does not need to be the best mathematician or linguist in the cohort for the reference to be effective (though they might be). Resilience, determination, kindness and a willingness to help others are all valued qualities Admissions Officers look for in potential students.
- Answer the question: What makes this student stand out?
- Include specific examples of how a student engages in the learning environment.

9 | Writing University References and Supporting Application Essays

- Share stories from the classroom.
- Support the transcript; if the student is a B student, emphasise qualities other than 'being the best in the class'.
- Avoid generic statements that could apply to any student; nothing should be generic in a teacher recommendation.

Common issues with US references are:

- not enough specific detail about the student;
- too much detail about the content of the course;
- too much similarity between different students' references written by the same teacher;
- a lack of anecdotes or stories about the student's impact inside and outside the classroom.

> **Scenario**
>
> A teacher who is writing a US teacher reference in support of a Year 13 applicant asks you what are the expectations and requirements for a US teacher reference.

> **Suggestions**
>
> Have a set of internal resources with generic advice and links to best practice that you can share with the teacher. Keep this updated so that you do not have to reinvent the wheel each year. Recognise that many teachers are anxious to do the best job possible for students who have asked for their support. Do you have time to have a quick chat with the teacher or with a group of teachers who have similar questions? Building relationships with your colleagues and providing them with support can go a long way to creating a positive and collaborative culture within your school in which everyone is working towards the same goal of supporting students.

The counsellor reference to support US university applicants

This reference is usually written by a Form Tutor, US Adviser/college counsellor or other member of staff who knows the student well. **As with the teacher recommendations, students should never be shown the counsellor reference.**

US counsellor references can be thought of as a form of character reference in which a student's values, contribution to your school and wider community, as well as their academic and extracurricular pursuits, are all detailed.

The counsellor reference is also the place to detail any hardships the student has faced during their time with you. This might include, for example, having caring responsibilities within their family or medical issues (such as having surgery or any other long-term physical illnesses) that have affected a student's school attendance. Be cautious about including information about mental health issues in your reference; these are often much more complex than you will have sufficient room or understanding to adequately convey in this piece of writing. Never disclose or write about issues that a student has spoken to you about without the student's express permission, preferably in writing.

US counsellor references: key points to keep in mind.

- The entire reference should be around two A4 pages in length.
- Answer the question: What makes this student stand out?
- Include specific examples of how a student engages with and positively affects your school and wider community.
- Share stories from your interactions with them and from your colleagues' interactions with them.
- Avoid generic statements that could apply to any student.

PRACTICAL TOOLS AND TIPS

- In some settings, Form Tutors, a Head of Year or Head of Sixth Form write the entire reference using guidance provided from the US Advisers/college counsellors; the US counsellor then edits and augments these references. Decide what makes the most sense within your setting and communicate expectations and guidelines clearly to colleagues.
- Determine which members of staff are likely to be able to provide you with the detailed information you need to write this type of reference. This is likely to be someone with pastoral responsibility for the student such as a Form Tutor or Head of Year or a member of the boarding staff if you work in a boarding school; it could even be a sports coach if your student is particularly athletic.
- While the responsibility for writing the counsellor reference generally rests with the US team, you need to be able to gather information from other sources in order to present a compelling picture of your student.
- How can you gather this information? One option is to ask relevant colleagues to interview the student and to submit the information they have gathered to the US team to be turned into a counsellor reference. A template with interview questions is on the following page.

ASK THE STUDENT

1. When did you join the school/college? What is your background/context academically/culturally/personally?

2. What academic areas, subject or subjects do you particularly love?

GUIDANCE Ask the student to tell you about *three* different examples (coursework or a project/essay/piece of internal work) that the student is most proud of or found the most interesting to complete *and why.*

   1.
   2.
   3.

ASK THE STUDENT

3. Do the examples above feed into any particular aspirations you have for the future? If so, how?

4. What are you passionate about beyond academics? How does this manifest for you?

GUIDANCE This might be an expansion on a co-curricular or related activity or somewhere else in school – anywhere that their presence has made a real difference.

5. Give me at least one example of how you have made the most of your time at school. How have you contributed to our school community? What motivated you to be involved in this way?

GUIDANCE Tell us a story!

FORM TUTOR INPUT

1. Give us three words or phrases to describe this student.

   1.
   2.
   3.

2. Tell us about a time when they showed their true selves – it can be something that happened in school or during an activity you lead.

GUIDANCE We are looking for liftable stories that show who this student is.

3. Anything else you know as their Form Tutor that would help strengthen their reference

GUIDANCE *This reference would be incomplete if I didn't mention these things about this student. This could be something small or seemingly insignificant – anything that gives us a better sense of who the student is. Please provide us with liftable quotes/stories we could include in the reference.*

Uploading and sending documents to US universities: Common App, Bridge-U and Unifrog

There are many platforms that enable schools to send the required documents to universities. These include:

- The Common Application https://www.commonapp.org
- Bridge-U https://bridge-u.com
- Unifrog https://www.unifrog.org

Whichever platform you use, you should allow ample time to check, upload and send; do not underestimate the amount of time this can take. All of these platforms require students to have an account. Make sure you set aside time for students to create and populate their accounts, ideally while you are with them so that you are on hand to answer any questions they might have.

A link for your school to upload the required school documents is provided via an email that is sent out once the student inputs the recommender or counsellor's details.

Students will need to be given clear instructions regarding exactly what details they should input into whichever system you decide to use. We recommend using a standard school email address which all relevant members of staff who have responsibility for uploading documents can use, for example, usdocs@yourdomain.org or something similarly generic.

Early and Regular round applications

Sending Early US applications

It is important to understand the timings involved in the Early Admissions rounds of the US application process. British schools using an A level or IBDP curriculum will likely have completed their predictions process in good time for the University of Oxford and University of Cambridge deadlines in mid-October; this is good news for anyone processing early US applications, as that deadline tends to fall around two weeks after the Oxford and Cambridge ones. In order to ensure that the school side of the documents is created, checked, uploaded and sent before the November deadline, you are likely to need to complete this work prior to half-term, which generally falls during or just after the mid-October deadline. This should mean that your US candidates will have their predictions well in time for the Early round.

Decide in advance what your policy will be regarding the submission of US documents. If you have a small cohort, you may choose to create and check all documents and wait to upload and send them during the last few days of the half-term. If you are managing a much larger cohort, you will need to be careful that you leave plenty of time for the document process to be completed.

In your first year, consider uploading and sending a set of students' documents early on. This will give you a sense of how long the process will take and what is involved. Plan to leave a minimum of 30 minutes per set of documents (transcript, two teacher references and one counsellor reference) when you come to the uploading and sending portion of the process. Keep in mind that you may also need to fill in a set of simple questions relating to each document that, although they are not complicated, take time to complete.

Sending Regular US applications

Some students will prefer not to commit to a university through an Early Decision application and will apply in the Regular round of applications, which are generally due around 1 January. The student may be hoping to receive an interview at the University of Oxford or University of Cambridge, be applying for an apprenticeship or Degree Apprenticeship with a later application timeline, or have financial aid needs that do not allow a commitment to a university under a binding plan.

You should plan to submit these students' documents before your term ends in December, but remember that you can submit their documents whenever they are ready. If you are managing a number of Early applications, you may consider waiting to work on Regular application documents until after the October half-term. One caveat: students might decide to apply Early when your school is on a break. If this happens and you are not able to submit the school documents for them on or before the deadline, do not worry. Most (if not all) university admissions departments allow for some flexibility in terms of submission of documents. Submit the documents as soon as possible after the student deadline and follow up with an email to your region's Admissions Officer or to the university's general admissions email address if appropriate. Ensure that students and parents have been made aware that many US universities allow a grace period for schools to submit documents; universities understand that counsellors are unlikely to be sending documents on New Year's Day when many deadlines fall. This should ensure that you do not receive emails when school is closed from panicked students and parents who are worried the student's application will not be considered because of missing documents. As long as the student submits their documents on time, you should not have an issue. It can take over a week for documents to be marked as received in students' application portals.

The US application essay and supplemental essays: Helping students manage the writing process

US application essays are tricky things to write; unlike UCAS personal statements, in which a student is making a case for study on a particular course, US essays tend to be centred around the candidate as a person. This type of writing can be very difficult for students, and they often need a considerable amount of help pushing through what can be an uncomfortable process. Empathy is key here, especially when a student is sharing stories that are important to them with you.

One key thing to be aware of: students often write deeply personal things in their US university application essays. You have a responsibility to honour that student's right to privacy by not discussing their work with, for example, their parents or other students or colleagues without their permission but also to be alert to potential safeguarding concerns. If you get any sense that a student is using their application essays to divulge a safeguarding issue, you must speak with your safeguarding lead.

Most students writing Common Application essays (or personal essays if the university is not on the Common App) write between four and eight drafts before finalising the essay. The essay titles for the Common App are updated every year but do not generally change significantly. The titles for 2024–5 can be found here: https://appsupport.commonapp.org/applicantsupport/s/article/What-are-the-2024-25-Common-App-essay-prompts

Students drafting the Common App essay or equivalent generally go through a series of drafts, with five to eight drafts typical for students who are committed to the process. You can help students start and work through the drafting process, which typically follows the following pattern:

Draft 1: idea;
Draft 2: build on the idea or restart;

Draft 3: finalise basic idea and build on it;
Draft 4: tease out themes; ensure the messaging is clear;
Draft 5–8: minor corrections.

Supplements tend to work in the same way. With all writing, students should be encouraged to draft and redraft until they are happy that the writing represents them, their vision and their mission. It should never be written in any part by an Adviser, external counsellor or AI.

Offering students feedback on writing

There are many ways to manage the feedback process for students. Putting a structure in place with clear deadlines is essential. Students who do not meet the deadlines set may have to accept that they will receive less feedback and support due to their own procrastination. Parents should be advised of this. Do not be tempted to help 'just one student' over the school holidays if you have put a policy in place that states that the school or college is closed and no feedback will be given. It is important to be fair to all students.

Beware of simply using email to give students feedback on their writing; versions can easily be confused or emails missed that can lead to confusion as to which version or set of feedback a student should be working on. Working within the Cloud using an online notebook such as Microsoft's OneNote or Google Classroom (and Google Docs) can work well as long as students have been given clear instructions as to how to label and share each successive draft. If your school uses Unifrog, the Common App tool allows students to request feedback from their assigned teachers/Advisers and for all parties to see each successive draft.

Helping students stay motivated

Intrinsic motivation is undoubtedly the best type of motivation a student can have in this process. However, students may have many reasons for applying to the US. Often, external pressures have also come to play in their decision to go to the US. This might be related to parental expectation, peer pressure or any other number of factors that mean they are relying on extrinsic motivation to get them through the process.

Your role is to identify why the student is applying to the US, which will allow you to tailor your approach to each student. Some may need more one-to-one attention; others may need your support in negotiating a university pathway plan with their parents; still others will happily and enthusiastically get on with the job in hand without needing or wanting much of your time. Each student is different, and you will need to be able to change your approach to students based on why they are making their applications so that you can offer the correct support. Students who have been given the information and tools required to take control of and ownership over the application process are often those who are the most motivated. You can help them by ensuring they have what they need to make informed and positive choices at every step.

Admissions representatives and their insights

Students are often desperate to understand exactly what they need to say or do to convince a university to accept them. Part of your job is to gently but firmly move them away from this line of thinking. There is no magic formula for getting into any specific university; if there were, everyone would be using it.

Many university admissions departments host podcasts, write blogs and run online seminars detailing what, to them, makes a compelling application. Some communications, such as counsellor emails and online meetings, are not intended for students, but quite a lot of communication is, and you should encourage students to proactively engage with this information. For example:

Yale

The Yale Admissions podcast has some useful advice for students on essays and supplements and how to respond to the specific questions on the Yale application.

They also have an episode on what to ask admissions representatives when they tour schools or host university fairs.

'Inside the Yale Admissions Office: College Search 101: How to Ask Questions'

Johns Hopkins

Essays that worked

https://apply.jhu.edu/college-planning-guide/essays-that-worked/

MIT

https://mitadmissions.org/blogs/

University of California

Extensive information about how to approach the Personal Insight questions

https://admission.universityofcalifornia.edu/how-to-apply/applying-as-a-freshman/personal-insight-questions.html

> **Scenario**
>
> A parent contacts you during the December holiday asking that you provide additional support to their daughter with her US application essays during the holiday period. Their email copies in other members of staff. What do you do?

> **Suggestions**
>
> - Anticipate such a situation and ensure you have clarified with Senior Management what the expectations are in terms of working when school is closed. You should have a policy which sets out clearly whether enquiries about US applications will be answered during holiday periods and the timescale for this.
> - Ensure that your school policy has been clearly communicated to parents and students multiple times.
> - Make sure you set an out-of-office detailing your policy so that parents and students have received a reply, even if it is not specific to their enquiry. Include general guidance about where students can find information about common issues, which can be both internal (for example, on your school's intranet) or external (for example, a link to the help section of the Common App website).
> - Consider whether you need to respond to the parent directly. Will your out-of-office suffice or is this a genuine emergency that requires a response? A response to an email often engenders further correspondence; a frustrated parent might communicate in a way that you find upsetting and would need support in responding to. If school is closed, you are unlikely to be able to rely on other colleagues to help or support you with this parent.
> - If you are expected to work during the holiday, set clear parameters around this. For example, you might set aside (and publicise to students) that you will be available on one or more specific days during the holiday period for emergency enquiries only.

Looking ahead: Key takeaways and questions to consider

- *Staff.* The three US references are confidential and should not be shared with the student or their parents. How will your school communicate your policy to students and parents?

- *Students.* Students need to be able to communicate with their US counsellor over an extended period of time, in order for their counsellor to write a meaningful and substantial reference for them based on their distinctive academic strengths and interests, their character, attributes and skills, and their unique impact and contribution to your school or college community and so on. How will you ensure appropriate additional material is available to counsellors in order to allow them to write effective references? How will you organise and manage the process of students nominating teachers to write an academic reference in support of their application? How will students be able to communicate their unique profile to US counsellors (via individual meetings, forms etc.)?

10 | Communication with students and staff

Higher Education Advisers play a crucial role in schools. In this chapter, we discuss effective communication between students, staff, parents, Senior Management and governors. From teachers advising students on their options to staff administering the application process to Form Tutors writing university references to Heads of Department or other managers building a team of staff, clear communication in your school community is key to running a successful and well-managed student programme.

This chapter will cover:

- effective communication with students;
- communication with teachers and other relevant colleagues;
- communication with senior leaders;
- communication with Form Tutors;
- how staff can manage and inspire different year groups.

Effective communication with students

Communication with individual students is always your priority; your primary role is to support and advise students about their future options and to keep an open dialogue with them. There will be various opportunities for whole-year group communication, from assemblies and smaller group meetings to individual meetings. Whether in a group or individual meeting, it is important to communicate clearly and accurately with students and treat them as adults with agency to help them make decisions about their future. University entry is not just the end of school; it is the beginning of a new chapter for students, marking the transition from school to university.

That said, schools expect students to make decisions about their future when students themselves may not have had much opportunity to do so until this point in their lives. This may be their first time being asked to consider what may turn out to be a vitally important life decision. It is crucial that, whatever decision is made, they themselves feel *they* have made it and that they recognise they must take responsibility for the consequences of that choice. A golden rule is not to tell them what to do so they feel the decision has been taken out of their hands. Encourage them to explore the possibilities and to keep an open mind. Above all, be supportive and positive, but at the same time try to make applicants appreciate the importance of their need to make *realistic* choices. This can be a difficult line to tread and becomes easier with experience. Above all, students need to make 'an informed decision'.

Given the high stakes involved, communication with students needs to be clear, timely and helpful. It should be planned and managed so that students understand what support you offer and when. There will be school holidays when your school is closed, and you are not available; students (and, depending on your school, parents as well) need to have this communicated to them well in advance.

> **QUESTIONS TO CONSIDER**
>
> - Consider how you might communicate to students in these settings: (a) Year group assembly, (b) group meetings or form time, (c) lecture slots, (d) via email or letters, (e) school intranets and (f) school social media (if applicable). Which messages are best suited to each individual context?
> - When are the key communication dates for sharing your information and advice? How will you communicate the following: (a) the introduction to your programme, (b) the support available during school hours, (c) what students are doing or should be doing, (d) university updates or changes to the application process and (e) the school's availability and service when public exam results are published.

> **Scenario**
>
> Lunch break on a Friday. 'I've got a question. Do you have a moment?' A Year 13 student sees that you are at your desk marking, and you reply, 'Of course, come in. Have a seat.' You put your pen down, ready to be fully engaged with this student. 'How can I help?' The student continues, 'I'm applying for Economics at UCL, University of Oxford, and LSE, but I also want to apply for PPE at Durham University and Edinburgh – how can my Personal Statement work for both?'
> What advice do you give?

Suggestions

- Offer them advice there and then. Suggest that they apply for either Economics at all five or PPE at all five. (Durham is the exception that will accept a substitute personal statement.)
- Advise them on their university choices and mention that these are five very competitive options, and they could consider one or two more 'Insurance' choices.
- Suggest that they look at the UCAS historic entry data tool based on their grades to find out about the success rate of previous applicants (see Chapter 11).
- Arrange to see them the next day at a mutually convenient time.
- Email their Form Tutor and ask the Form Tutor to follow up.
- Find them some personal statement examples for Economics and PPE.

Some schools will allow students to 'drop in'; others may have a booking system. This student has taken the time to come and see you, and they deserve an answer, even if it is incomplete or part of an ongoing conversation. Making time for students when they seek your advice is one of the best ways to build positive relationships with students and the wider cohort. If you have time, we suggest that you try to deal with their question then and there and then follow up as needed. Often, a little input or reassurance from you can go a long way. Also, consider having specified times for quick queries with an option to book an appointment for further discussion.

Follow up

Make sure you keep notes from meetings with individual students, particularly if you anticipate future difficulties with them or their parents. If appropriate, taking notes during the meeting is often the most efficient way to record what you and the student have discussed. If you have time, explain to the student what you are doing and that you will send the notes on to them at the end of the meeting. Often, this allows students to take in more of what you are saying to them as they are not worried about remembering every detail. These notes can be extremely helpful later in the process or when speaking to colleagues or parents about a student's plans or progress in their applications. You will find that you often answer the same questions repeatedly, and it may be that you have a standard piece of advice you can insert into your notes when scenarios like the one above present themselves.

> Depending on your school's organisation, you may find it useful to email these notes to the student and their Form Tutor immediately after the meeting, especially if you have given advice that the student is likely to need further support in either coming to terms with or enacting.

> **PRACTICAL TOOLS AND TIPS**
>
> If your school subscribes to Unifrog, you can record this as an interaction that the Form Tutor will also be able to see. You should use the procedure for noting this on school records to share with other colleagues, as appropriate.

Plans and timelines

Examples of different types of communication you are likely to need to make are below. Consider how you will share this information:

- reports for governors and senior leaders on university entry outcomes;
- university destination lists for marketing and school magazines;
- school publications and letters to parents about the programme – any forthcoming events, updates and the support available in school;
- staff updates on the changing HE landscape, the university selection process, the expectations of students and what is required of staff;
- student assemblies, timelines and deadlines, whole group meetings, smaller meetings and individual meetings.

Communication with teachers and other relevant colleagues

Higher Education advice requires professional expertise, but often it is done in a context where teachers have multiple commitments, as well as limited time and resources. Your biggest assets in any school setting are your colleagues. While you know what is technically required of students in terms of their applications, they know the students pastorally and academically. Do not underestimate just how helpful accessing and using that knowledge appropriately can be.

Schools and colleges are, obviously, busy places, and while university applications are very important, help with them is just one part of a teacher's workload. In order to maximise the support you receive from teaching staff, helping with a student's application should be made as easy and as appropriately scheduled as possible; teachers should be given both support and, crucially, time to complete any work you ask of them.

Consider what staff are doing at each point in the year. Are they invigilating and marking mock exams? Writing reports? Running activities? You are far more likely to engender feelings of goodwill from your colleagues and to have your request promptly fulfilled if you avoid asking staff members to produce this work during their busiest times.

> **QUESTIONS TO CONSIDER**
>
> - Think about the management structure in your school context – which staff members have the responsibility for university applications?
> - Consider how you might communicate with teachers in the following settings: (a) whole staff meetings, (b) department meetings, (c) email or letters and (d) school intranets.
> - When are the key communication dates? How will you communicate to colleagues the following: (a) your programme, (b) the part they play in the application process and (c) any information, advice or training on university reference writing?
> - Reflect on what effective communication with staff looks like in your context. Conversely, think about what can go wrong and how this could be mitigated.

Communication with senior leaders

The stakes are high for Senior Leadership Teams. The responsibility of staff advising students on their future choices cannot be underestimated. University destination lists play an important role in data analysis for governors and for school marketing. A typical question from any parent visiting a school is, 'Where do your students go on to study? What proportion go on to (a) the University of Oxford or University of Cambridge, (b) or Russell Group universities and (c) Ivy League universities in the US?' How you communicate and present this information is very important.

> **PRACTICAL TOOLS AND TIPS**
>
> Update other members of staff and senior leaders regarding university entry results. Consider the following:
>
> - Keep good records. You should be able to accurately and quickly access information about the cohort's university entry results as a whole and those of individual students. Consider how you might collect and collate this information. You may wish to use a system such as Bridge-U or Unifrog to track student applications and results; depending on the size of your school, a set of spreadsheets for staff to use may be more appropriate.
> - Who and which school departments need to be informed about university entry results, and when? For example, your Head may wish to include results in an end-of-term or beginning-of-term communication to the wider school community. Your marketing team may want information at specific points in the year; for example, early US university application outcomes and Oxford and Cambridge outcomes can usually be announced at the same time in January. Will this take the form of an article, a brief summary of results, letter or another type of communication?
> - When will your governors expect to be informed about the results?
>
> US universities: In the middle of the cycle (as above)? At the end, when all offers are known (between April and mid-May)?
>
> UK universities: For the UK, they may want to know about UCAS offers as they come in from October to June, or at the end of the cycle in August/September when students are placed at university.
>
> Make sure that you have a system in place to collate this information so that it is easily accessible and available for you when you are asked to produce a summary of university entry results.

Communication with Form Tutors

Form Tutors manage groups of students and have insight into both their academic and pastoral lives at school, as well as their health history, any learning differences, domestic backgrounds and family affairs. This information is invaluable when writing references and can be very useful when advising students on university pathways if you are working as part of a small team or on your own.

If you are part of a larger team of staff, you may find that you can gather the information you need about a student's circumstances in your termly or yearly meetings with students. Still, gathering basic information on students from their Form Tutors prior to meeting with students can give you very useful knowledge on which you can base your advice when you meet with the students themselves, as well as ensure relevant information (such as mitigating circumstances) is included in the reference.

How staff can manage and inspire different year groups

At every stage, staff need to encourage young people to think positively about their future options. At all times, they should try to help students keep an open mind about their career choices, encourage them to be proactive and take responsibility for their futures.

Your colleagues are likely to have valuable insights and personal experiences that you can draw on to strengthen your programme. Try to create a whole-school culture of positive thinking and excitement about students' futures. A few ways to involve other members of staff might include:

- **Subject-specific advice.** Members of staff with particular interest or experience in specific academic areas may want to advise on that particular subject. For example, the Head of Economics could be qualified to advise students on their university applications in that subject area. Make sure that their contribution to your programme is acknowledged in the school timetable or club/society rota.
- **Careers and professional insight.** Encourage staff members with industry experience to speak to students about their pathways; students do not always realise that there are many ways, through their university and course choices, to get to the same workplace.
- **Staff participation.** Asking younger members of staff who have left university in the past 5–10 years to take part in a panel discussion to answer questions and outline key aspects of their university experience to a group of students.

UK context

- Students at the beginning of secondary school (Years 7, 8 and 9) can encounter information that relates to the Gatsby Benchmarks in PSHE lessons, through attendance at careers events or university fairs held at school, or through assemblies specifically

- addressing post-school options. All teachers can also address Gatsby Benchmark 4 (Linking Curriculum Learning to Careers) in lessons as appropriate.
- Year 10 and 11 advice tends to focus on Sixth Form subject choices – such as A level, T level, BTEC or IB subjects.
- Year 12 advice focuses more on exploring post-18 options (see Chapter 1), including apprenticeships, employment, education and training. For students applying to university, it could cover how to choose a UCAS course, how to make a competitive application, such as the quality of a personal statement, and any admissions test or interview preparation.
- Year 13 focuses on how to make a competitive application (see Chapter 2), whether for a job, an apprenticeship or training. For university applicants, it involves completing a UCAS application, choosing Firm and Insurance offers and reminders such as applying for accommodation, student finance and so on. There could be a focus on mock interviews for applicants to apprenticeships or some universities.

Looking ahead: Key takeaways and questions to consider

- *Students.* **Communication with students should always be positive and support their wellbeing.** Think about the necessity and frequency of your communications with students in terms of (a) the whole-year group and (b) individual students. What is the most effective way of communicating with your students in your particular setting?

- *Staff.* **Your collaboration with staff is essential. Staff often play a key role in university admissions, and you depend on them for drafting and supplying material for university references etc.** Think about the necessity and frequency of your communications with teachers and staff in terms of (a) the whole staff body and (b) other staff meetings.

- *Senior Leaders.* **Typically, senior leaders need to convey information and updates to governors.** When do you need to communicate information about applications or outcomes? What level of detail is appropriate (for example, statistics, summaries or analysis of trends)?

11 | Managing expectations

In this chapter, we deal with questions about the expectations of parents or guardians and students. We discuss the responsibilities of students in relation to their applications, the role of parents and the role of the school or college. It is important to encourage students to know themselves and follow their interests and passions, but some may feel under pressure from their peers, parents or societal expectations. We outline some scenarios and how to respond to issues that might arise from parent and staff roles and student responsibilities. We also cover how to support students in making their transition from school or college to work or further study.

This chapter will cover:

- *expectations and parenting styles;*
- *how schools and colleges can work with parents;*
- *expectations, plans and university;*
- *the expectations of students, teachers and Advisers;*
- *communication with parents.*

Expectations and parenting styles

Anette Lareau, the sociologist, in her book *Unequal Childhoods*, outlines different models of parenting: 'concerted cultivation', a parenting style where children require constant care and training by adults, to the more relaxed approach of 'natural growth parenting'. These different approaches to parenting will affect how parents interact with their child during the application process, whether they are applying for jobs, apprenticeships, Degree Apprenticeships or university. On the other hand, if parents are uninterested, uninvolved or unavailable, students will rely on the support of their school or college.

In his book, *The Anxious Generation: How the Great Rewiring of Childhood Is Causing an Epidemic of Mental Illness*, Jonathan Haidt uses the analogy of racing cars to illustrate the approach that some parents take towards university admissions. The child is like a fragile racing car, and the parents are like the pit crew, responsible for the fine-tuning of 'the race car', which depends on their pit stop team for success.

Paradoxically, this approach taken by parents can become problematic if it prevents their son or daughter from 'owning the application process'. If students are constantly micromanaged by a parent, the risk is that they won't find the independence they need to develop as adults (in the workplace or at university). There are examples outlined in this article from as far back as 2007: https://www.bu.edu/articles/2007/the-really-long-good-bye-helicopter-parents-in-the-college-years/.

Autonomy is key to the success of university applications, and students should be 'the drivers' of their own application without the need for excessive pit stop intervention from their parents. Arguably, parents should give plenty of encouragement, stay open to the possibilities and be open-minded about the outcome or final university destination.

There is an important distinction between advising and influencing. Our task in schools is to present students with a range of options. Members of the Career Development Institute abide by the CDI code of ethics that requires 'impartial' Careers guidance and encourages students to make 'autonomous' decisions.

https://www.thecdi.net/about-us/cdi-code-of-ethics

Above all, parents and schools should encourage and allow students to be *active* in their research, course choice, Open Day visits and university choices. A university or job application is not something that happens to a student; their university, apprenticeship or job applications are something that they are hopefully excited about and feel responsible for.

How schools and colleges can work with parents

None of this is to say that parents should not be involved in their children's university applications. However, they may need clear guidance from you as to how that involvement can remain helpful, healthy and productive. For example, you might organise an information session for parents at the end of Year 11 in which you detail what careers and university guidance you offer to students in the Sixth Form, the timeline for this guidance and how parents and guardians can help support students. Consider working with your Sixth Form and Head of PSHE to tie this to a wider conversation about supporting students in all aspects of their school or college life. There is a fine line between support and pressure. Encourage parents to question where they are getting their information from and how current it is.

Useful resources to share with parents:

https://www.ucas.com/discover/advice-parents-guardians-and-carers
https://childmind.org/article/helping-kids-make-decisions/
https://www.rochester.edu/newscenter/parents-guardians-influence-college-admissions-process-541502/

These are possible ways to help parents have access to information about university admissions and other post-18 options:

- Information booklets and FAQs. These can be produced and updated on an annual basis and shared with students at appropriate times:
  - For Year 11 parents, a booklet on Sixth Form options, KS5 qualifications, subject choices and post-16 options. This is an excellent resource on choosing A level subjects and equivalents, published by the Russell Group: https://www.informedchoices.ac.uk.
  - For Year 12 parents, a booklet on post-18 options, including apprenticeships, entrepreneurship, Gap Years, the UK, the US and international university admissions.
  - For Year 13 parents, information about student finance and how students can choose between university offers.
- Invite parents to participate in a careers fair, where they can share their expertise with current students.
- Run information sessions for parents online and host Higher Education evenings with representatives from various universities.
- Regular communication with parents via letters and emails containing relevant information and reminders and letting them know how frequent this will be.

PRACTICAL TOOLS AND TIPS

- Assumptions about families should be avoided. In your emails, letters and other communications, consider how you will address your audience: 'parents and carers' or 'parents and guardians'. Also consider how you will refer to their children, 'daughters and sons'.
- If a student's relationship with both of their parents or carers has irreconcilably broken down, they can share this with universities. On the student's UCAS application in the 'More About You' section, they can indicate if they are 'estranged' from their parents: applying to university if you are experiencing estrangement.
- https://www.ucas.com/applying/applying-university/individual-needs/estranged-students

Scenario

A parent contacts you to ask for advice about their son's application near the end of Year 12. They have already discussed their son's predicted grades with the school. They now contact you to ask about his university choices. You meet them and they ask for bespoke data based on students applying from your school (for three specific degree courses) for the last five years, believing that this information is critical before their son decides on his degree course. What do you do?

Suggestions

The parent has asked you for data to help their son make an informed decision. This may seem like a reasonable request; however, it is problematic in various ways:

- The data they want is not immediately available, and it would be time-consuming to produce it.
- The data they are requesting may be difficult to produce: there are multiple factors that determine the success of an application, including GCSE or equivalent grades, predicted grades, personal statement, admissions tests and interview performance (if applicable).

Follow up

Before responding to requests for large amounts of information, which will be time-consuming for you to put together (for the benefit of one particular student), discuss this with the most relevant colleague, such as their Form Tutor, Head of Year or a senior member of staff, as appropriate.

Parents in these situations are often looking for reassurance that a member of staff is engaged with their child's application. Anxious parents often feel better after a short phone call in which reassurance and understanding, as well as some general advice, are offered. These conversations are most successful if you have recently also spoken to their child. The majority of parents are very receptive to receiving information from the school and eager to build positive relationships with staff.

You could also communicate these points:
- Explain that university destination lists are publicly available on the school website but are of limited use. The trends and patterns based on university destinations from previous years do not shed light on the factors that influenced the offers made; hence, 'our policy is that we don't supply bespoke reports of this kind'.
- It is appropriate to focus on the selection criteria for their son, who is applying now. If he is also applying to the US, the success of his application will be dependent on the strength of his personal Common App essay, supplementary essays and fit with the university.
- Encourage the student and his parent to consider what the student can do now in terms of his super-curricular activities and developing his academic profile, ready to make a competitive application. The focus of their research should be on course choice and course content.

Scenario

A Year 12 student tells you they would like to apply for English and Drama, but they explain that their parents believe it would be a waste of time and will only allow them to study Law, Medicine or Engineering at university. They also mention that their parents will only allow them to apply to the University of Oxford, or the University of Cambridge and the London colleges, such as Imperial College London and UCL. How do you advise them?

Suggestions

Follow up with their Form Tutor to discuss what is appropriate in the circumstances, whether a phone call or email to the parents or a discussion on this topic at the next parents' evening.

- The strength of a university or course 'brand' can influence its perceived prestige. Acknowledge that for some parents, there is some perceived prestige involved.
- Point them in the direction of the Key Information Set (KIS) data: https://discoveruni.gov.uk so they can compare courses and consider alternatives. Also, the highfliers report of graduate employment shows that most employers don't specify a degree subject.

- Explain that every student should make their own informed choices and control the application process, including choosing the course they apply for. They are more likely to succeed if they apply for a course that interests them.
- If they are interested in London as a location, there are over 40 universities and Higher Education Institutions to choose from. If the student wants to study English and Drama, they should consider the course that offers the most appeal or variations, such as English and Theatre Studies at the University of Warwick. They should compare the English courses available and where the combination of English and Drama is available: for example, the University of Exeter, University of East Anglia, Manchester, Greenwich and so on. If they are interested in London, they could also consider single honours English at KCL or London Northeastern. English at UCL is renowned for providing one-to-one tutorials (in addition to seminars and lectures), made possible by the relatively small cohort of students who are admitted to this prestigious course each year.

Expectations, plans and university

Some students may only want to apply for a 'prestigious' university or course as a stepping stone to a graduate job. Given the cost of a university education, some parents might assume that only certain courses and universities are value for money or 'worth it'. In short, parents are only willing for their daughter or son to attend 'university x' or 'course y'. The rationale given is often 'in the best interest' of the student. However, it is more advisable to allow a student to have a free hand to choose the course and university that they believe they are best suited to. Increasingly, the name of the university is less significant as graduate recruiters can screen out university names in their selection process; it is important that students are proactive and build their skills, experience and CV while at university.

Schools and colleges play a role in managing the expectations of students and parents: a clear policy should exist on predicted grades and helping students make appropriate choices. If they are applying to university, they should have some 'aspirational', 'solid' and 'safe' options included. What we say and how we advise are crucial and key factors that shape student choices. However, it is the students' decision to go to university, and your responsibility is to encourage them to make an informed choice and evaluate their options. If their Plan A doesn't work out, do they have a Plan B or C in place? Have they considered whether university is the best option for them, and if not, how can you help them explore alternatives?

The expectations of students, teachers and Advisers

Teachers are responsible for ensuring the students' success in their particular subjects. Often, this takes the form (as it should) of encouragement and positive feedback. Students can sometimes take this, along with strong predictions, as a sign that they are more likely than others to obtain a place studying that subject at university. Teachers and Advisers can tactfully remind students to keep this in perspective:

- Academic grades are necessary, but they are not necessarily sufficient and meeting the minimum requirements does not guarantee an offer.
- A successful application depends on multiple factors beyond academic grades. Many students need to understand selection processes and take control of the elements that they are responsible for.
- Students may be strong in their school or college cohort; however, they are one among many exceptional students in the national and global application pool.

Statistics

The use of statistics can be helpful, so students understand the data and the level of competition for places (such as acceptance rates, also known as 'admit rates', and any other objective information supplied by the universities themselves).

For example, a recent University of Oxford annual report showed the most competitive courses: 20 applicants per place for Computer Science, 19.7 for Economics and Management and 12.8 for Mathematics and Computer Science.

By sharing these statistics, you are not implying the student is not worthy of a place or that they will or will not obtain one; you are showing them that, on balance, the statistical likelihood of them gaining a place may be smaller than they understood, so having a Plan B or Plan C is advisable. You can encourage them to make their application as competitive as possible so it stands out in a highly selective pool of applicants. Students can also see which courses are 'less popular': for example, at most universities, there are fewer applicants per place for Modern Languages, Archaeology and Classics. However, students should avoid applying for courses where they think their chances of admission are higher; their genuine interest in the course they are applying for is essential.

University of Oxford: https://www.ox.ac.uk/about/facts-and-figures/admissions-statistics

University of Cambridge:
https://www.undergraduate.study.cam.ac.uk/apply/statistics
https://www.undergraduate.study.cam.ac.uk/sites/www.undergraduate.study.cam.ac.uk/files/publications/ug_admissions_statistics_2023_cycle.pdf

UCAS historic entry grades data

As part of their research, students can use the historic entry grades data. It is important that they understand all elements of the selection process: academic grades are just one part. However, they can discover more about offer rates for their course for previous students who took A level and Pearson BTEC Level 3 National Extended Diplomas. The data shows what percentage of students with the same grades were successful in gaining a place, based on previous data. It is important they understand that the percentage shown is not an indication of their likelihood of getting an offer in the current admissions cycle – it is only an indication of how many students who had similar grades in the past secured an offer. Furthermore, they should use this tool with caution.

- Entry grades from 2017 to 2019 may be different for specific courses today.
- Typical entry grades are not the same as entry requirements and should not be relied upon as such.
- They only show A level grades and not grades for the IB or other equivalent qualifications.

UCAS understanding entry requirements:

https://www.ucas.com/applying/you-apply/what-and-where-study/ucas-undergraduate-entry-requirements

UCAS historic entry grades/offer rate calculator:

https://www.ucas.com/applying/you-apply/what-and-where-study/entry-requirements/understanding-historical-entry-grades-data

Scenario

A student with very strong predicted grades is applying to five universities that are all 'safer' choices, given that they comfortably exceed the requirements by a considerable margin at all of them. They have included no 'aspirational' or 'solid' choices, only 'safer' options. How would you advise them?

Suggestions

This student may have put in place some parameters for their university search that you don't yet understand. For example, a student from a specific region may not feel confident or be financially able to study away from home. Sometimes health, mental health or simply preference for certain surroundings might also come into play. For example, some students don't like cities while others really want to be in a big city centre. Studying locally is preferable for students who prefer to go home at weekends or keep jobs near home.

Asking questions here, rather than making suggestions as to why a student may have chosen the universities they have, is one way to approach the situation and get the information you are seeking.

Try to ascertain why they have chosen those universities. You might start by praising the fact that they have made a list at all, noting that this can often be a difficult process for students. Be curious. Listen to what they are saying. Ask them what they like about these universities and listen to what they tell you. Perhaps they have chosen courses they think sound exciting; perhaps they are keen to study abroad; maybe they want to be based in a certain region.

Perhaps they don't feel confident about their academic performance and would benefit from mentoring by a member of staff. Encourage them to speak to their Form Tutor, Head of Year or Head of Sixth Form if you feel they need pastoral or academic support. Make sure that you follow up with another member of staff who has pastoral responsibility for that student to ensure they are receiving any help they need.

Communication with parents

Parents and carers often play a large part in their child's university applications. It is important to be aware of the potential issues that can arise when communicating with parents.

Occasionally you may be thanked for your work or praised when a student receives a university offer. Keep these emails. Equally, expect to receive emails from disappointed students and parents. However, avoid the traps of assuming either that the student's university place is your achievement or that it is your fault when a student is disappointed. This underlines the need to ensure that the student and the parent feel the original choice of course and institution was the applicant's alone. Moreover, the highly selective nature of university admissions means that talented and capable students who have a flawless academic track record might face their first-ever setback if they are rejected by a university of their choice. Your focus should be on the wellbeing of the student concerned.

Reflect on how you might respond to these emails, either praising or blaming the school for an application outcome. If you are new to the role, you will find with time that similar situations and emails come up year after year.

Make sure that any response you send reflects the values, context and acceptable style of your school and is not inflammatory, aggressive, over-defensive or emotionally driven. Remember that email is a blunt, one-dimensional tool of communication, and its tone or content may easily be misinterpreted. Initial contact may be better made by phone call, which may then be followed up by an email confirming what you had agreed upon by the end of your phone discussion. Disappointed parents can sometimes communicate in unconstructive ways. If you find yourself feeling defensive or upset by parental communication, it is wise to send a holding email to give yourself more time to consider how best to respond. If you are still unsure, speak to a senior leader who should be able to advise and support you.

You may wish to keep a file containing examples of how you handled difficult situations. Review these at the start of the year to remind yourself of common issues that might arise. You can also use an anonymised version of these scenarios in staff training.

11| Managing Expectations

> **Scenario**
>
> A student or parent contacts you by email during the school holidays. They insist that they need to speak with you during the break and that they require documents or references to be provided to universities while school is closed.

> **Suggestions**
>
> - Why do they need to speak to you? Is this truly an emergency, or can the matter wait until the start of term?
> - What are your school policies regarding contact between teaching staff, students and parents during school breaks?
> - What is your school's policy regarding contact with staff during breaks? Have you communicated this clearly to your students?

If you have a large cohort of US and international applicants, some deadlines or the release of decisions may happen during or just after a break. Decide in advance of the start of your programme with your next cohort what your policy is regarding supporting university applications during the school holidays.

Keep in mind that many parents and students spend school breaks working on university applications and may expect that you will do the same. However, it is important for your and your colleagues' wellbeing, as well as that of your students, that you all take breaks at appropriate points in the year.

If you have made it unequivocally clear in past correspondence that you are not available between specific dates in the school holiday, and you receive an email within those dates, you are under no obligation to reply to this request until the end of your absence period.

- You may wish to set aside particular days during holidays when you will be available by email or online to help students with last-minute queries.
- However, it cannot be the *whole* of the school holidays. Inform parents in writing of the specific dates you are available.
- Alternatively, you may maintain a policy of no contact during the school holidays.

Whatever you decide works best in your school context, you must communicate this to students and their parents in advance. Telling is one thing, writing another. Be aware of the pitfalls of 'just answering one email'; if you have told your cohort that you are unavailable during the school holidays but then provide support to one or a small group of students anyway, you are opening yourself and other staff up to potential accusations of unfairness. Make sure that all members of staff are aware of the school policy and adhere to it.

Students and parents talk to other parents and students and often compare notes; they can be especially sensitive to perceived unfairness, so you may find that not following your own stated policy causes resentment and difficulties. You may find that if you break your own no-contact or limited-contact policy during the October half-term but try to enforce it during the Christmas break, you will receive pushback from parents and students who see the policy as negotiable. Be clear, and above all, consistent in how you engage with students. Every student deserves the same level of service and help as every other, regardless of their parents' communication with you.

Frequently Asked Questions

What are the Frequently Asked Questions in your context (from students, teachers and parents)?

Consider:

- How will you respond to these enquiries? Emails? Phone calls? Both? Letter (more formal)?
- What are the common misunderstandings? How might you address these?
- What is the best forum in which you can address FAQs? Online live information sessions? Pre-recorded information sessions? In-person information sessions? Events with outside speakers? FAQs on your school website/intranet?
- You are likely to employ a mix of strategies to educate and inform your school community about Higher Education. Consider the character and culture of your parent and student body when planning events and information sessions. Are most parents local? International? How can you maximise your reach?

Looking ahead: Key takeaways and questions to consider

- *Students.* **Communication should always be positive and support students' wellbeing.** How can you and your colleagues ensure that your students feel empowered rather than pressured during the application process? Consider ways you can provide realistic but encouraging guidance that will help students explore their genuine interests.

- *Staff.* **Collaboration is essential in supporting university applications.** How can different staff members work together to provide comprehensive support? Consider how you will coordinate your efforts on behalf of your students among key members of staff (Form Tutors, subject teachers, Career Advisers and other relevant colleagues).

- *Senior Leaders.* **Develop school policies to help manage the expectations of students and parents.** How will you communicate your policies with students and parents to ensure that they have appropriate expectations? What do students and parents expect about the support available at your school? What is a reasonable level of support and advice for university applications? In your school or college setting, what expectations are there about the likelihood of university offers and outcomes? Consider how you might help students to have realistic expectations.

12 | The role of AI in university applications

Advances in the field of Artificial Intelligence, specifically Generative AI, *are a very fast-moving area that has already begun affecting educational practice across all stages of education. GenAI allows anyone to manage the creation of content which can take the form of text, videos, audio and images. At present, text can be created using Large Language Models (LLMs) such as ChatGPT, Gemini, DeepSeek or Claude. This technology, and its use in educational settings, calls for robust policies and guidelines for students. The aim of this chapter is to explore how schools can advise students on their use of AI and how they can understand the uses of AI by universities and employers. We consider the implications of this fast-moving technology for school/college policy and practice.*

This chapter will cover:

- understanding the fast-changing landscape and the impact of AI on education;
- implications of AI for school and college policies;
- university policies on the use of AI in undergraduate applications;
- students using AI for research;
- use of AI for ideas to support your work;
- AI and the future of admissions and selection processes.

Understanding the fast-changing landscape and the impact of AI on education

In 2015, Suskind and Suskind, in their book *The Future of the Professions*, predicted the decline of the professions and outlined the fast-changing nature of human expertise.

https://academic.oup.com/book/40589

The speed of developments in technology and AI means that schools struggle to keep up. It is not difficult to show a PowerPoint slide to parents indicating the World Economic Forum skills for 2030, but it is another thing to keep a school curriculum up to date so that it will prepare and equip students with the skills needed for jobs in the future.

https://www.weforum.org/focus/skills-for-your-future/

Anything specific we could meaningfully say about GenAI and its effect on education at present would likely be out of date by the time this book is published. However, what we can say with some certainty is that, like the calculator or the personal computer, GenAI is likely here to stay. Whether it becomes an asset or a liability largely depends on how we collectively manage its implementation and use.

At the moment, much of the discussion around GenAI in schools is centred around the concept of cheating and GenAI's potentially detrimental effects on students' ability to critically think and complete academic tasks without relying on Artificial Intelligence's assistance. University Admissions Officers and tutors seem to be taking a similar line with regards to using GenAI for personal statements and personal essays. However, we must stress that any stated policy from any institution is subject to change often and without notice. If you or your students are unsure what a university or other institution deems acceptable, you must seek out this information rather than just guessing what the policy might be.

Implications of AI for school and college policies

Throughout the university application process, students need to evaluate at each stage if using AI to complete aspects of their applications is appropriate. They will need clear guidance on academic honesty as to what is acceptable within their context. This will likely differ depending on the level of work it is being used for (homework versus coursework, for instance) and what the intended purpose of the work is.

One positive implication of AI in the context of education is a new approach to honesty and transparency in relation to citing sources and referencing. All schools need policies that outline what is acceptable use of AI and the consequences of its misuse.

On the other hand, there are risks involved; the University of Cambridge, in line with the Russell Group policy, makes clear that passing off text written by GenAI as your own work counts as academic misconduct. Students who become used to using GenAI in school may encounter difficulties when starting a course at a university that forbids it.

University policies on the use of AI in undergraduate applications

From A level, T level and BTEC to IB, every exam board will have a policy on the use of AI. Schools communicate these policies, and students are responsible for following them. Each university will have a policy on academic honesty and the use of AI in university applications.

University of Cambridge advice for undergraduates:

https://www.undergraduate.study.cam.ac.uk/apply/ai-and-undergraduate-applications
https://www.cam.ac.uk/stories/ai-and-scholarship-manifesto

In the past, if a student needed help writing a UCAS personal statement or completing a coursework assignment, they would need to find someone who was willing to assist with or complete that work on their behalf. With GenAI, a student can ask an LLM to complete this work for them within a certain set of parameters, and the platform will oblige. For busy students in a hurry, they may be tempted to use it as a shortcut, or they may rationalise that the information they fed the LLM was 'theirs', and therefore the output of the LLM is likely to be similar to what they themselves would have written. However, having a justification for using it doesn't mean that the use is acceptable. Presenting an LLM's work or another person's work as your own, regardless of where the work originated, is problematic, and students should be aware that exam boards, universities and employers are sensitive to and on the lookout for the use of GenAI by candidates.

Using GenAI for UCAS personal statements

GenAI has the capacity to marshal large sets of data into easily digestible content; it is arguably a timesaver. However, our current view is that anything that students write and submit as their own work, whether UCAS personal statements, US essays or supplements, is best written by them alone. Given that it is the student voice that matters, we would recommend that students use their own words and not use it for any of the writing elements of a university application unless the body to which they are submitting their application explicitly permits or encourages it.

UCAS guidance on the use of AI for personal statements

UCAS is clear that copying and pasting from ChatGPT or any other LLM should be avoided and would count as cheating. However, they take the approach that it is a potential tool that, if 'used correctly might be acceptable, in three specific ways, including, for example to: a) generate ideas or a list of relevant skills b) to structure writing, c) to check for readability, phrasing and concision'. https://www.ucas.

com/applying/applying-university/writing-your-personal-statement/guide-using-ai-and-chatgpt-your-personal-statement

Common App guidance on use of AI

Common App, the college application tool used by 1,000 institutions nationwide, in August included a restriction on 'substantive' AI use in college admissions applications as part of its *fraud policy*. The addition was a response to feedback from member colleges and an internal desire to 'keep up with the changing technologies', a spokesperson wrote.

What does 'substantive' mean? Common App's CEO, Jenny Rickard, said there's no definition, and that's intentional, writing in an email that 'we will evaluate the totality of the circumstances to determine if a student truly intended to misrepresent content generated by AI technology as their own work'.

Common App doesn't determine whether students are being honest – that's up to the member colleges to figure out. But if Common App concludes that a student plagiarised, that student's account may be terminated, and Common App will notify the campuses to which the student applied, Rickard wrote. https://calmatters.org/education/higher-education/2023/10/college-application-essays/

Students using AI for research

LLMs and other GenAI tools can be helpful for students keen to fully research their university options at the start of their university application process. LLMs are able to tailor their responses to particular requests in a way that search engines cannot.

For example, you may be working with a student who is a high-level athlete; the student is interested in studying Management, Business or Sport Science at a university either in the UK or the US that has a well-ranked athletic programme for their sport. Where do you start in terms of advising the student?

Previously, you would have needed to look in multiple places to discover appropriate courses. For the UK, BUCS (British Universities and Colleges Sport); for the US, NCAA (the National Collegiate Athletics Association); individual US and UK university and college websites; UCAS.

However, by using an LLM, you can give yourself an easy starting point from which to continue your research with your student. Start with a prompt to Gemini (Google), such as: *I am helping a student who is a high-level swimmer (internationally ranked). The student is interested in studying Management, Business or Sport Science at a university either in the UK or the US that has a well-ranked athletic programme for their sport. Could you please make 10 suggestions as to the most appropriate courses for them to consider?*

As you and your student work together to narrow down the list, you can modify your original prompt or ask for clarification. You can type in more refined and specific prompts based on your student's preferences. This could relate to location, ranking of programmes (either sport or academic or both), league or division and so on. GenAI cannot provide complete answers, but it can be an extremely useful tool for counsellors working one-to-one with students.

An example of the response to the prompt above is below. You may want to use multiple sites and compare the results.

For example, Gemini elicited the following response:

University Options for a High-Level Swimmer Pursuing Business or Sport Science

Understanding the balance:

Before diving into specific universities, it is crucial to note that balancing elite-level swimming with rigorous academic studies requires exceptional time management and dedication. The student should be prepared for a demanding schedule.

Key factors:

- **Academic reputation.** *Strong programmes in Management, Business or Sport Science.*
- **Athletic excellence.** *A renowned swimming programme with a history of producing top-level athletes.*
- **Scholarship opportunities.** *Generous financial aid packages for student-athletes.*
- **Support system.** *Comprehensive athlete support services (e.g. academic advising, sports medicine and nutrition).*

Potential universities

United Kingdom:

1. **Loughborough University.** *Renowned for its sports science and strong swimming programme. Offers a variety of business degrees.*

2. **University of Bath.** Excellent reputation in sports science and management, with a world-class swimming facility.
3. **University of Stirling.** Strong in sports science and business, with a focus on athlete development.
4. **University of Liverpool.** Offers a good balance of business programmes and a competitive swimming team.
5. **University of Sheffield.** Strong academic programmes and a competitive swimming environment.

United States:

6. **University of California, Berkeley.** Offers top-tier business and sports science programmes, combined with a dominant swimming team.
7. **Stanford University.** Renowned for academics and athletics, with a strong tradition of swimming excellence.
8. **University of Texas, Austin.** Offers a large business school and a powerful swimming programme.
9. **Indiana University, Bloomington.** Known for its business school and strong swimming tradition.
10. **University of Southern California (USC).** Combines a prestigious business school with a competitive swimming team.

Additional considerations:

- **Research specific programmes.** Dive deeper into the curriculum, faculty and career outcomes of the chosen degrees.
- **Visit campuses.** If possible, visit the universities to experience the atmosphere and meet with coaches and academic advisers.
- **Consider the overall college experience.** Factors such as campus life, location and student culture should also be considered.
- **Explore other countries.** While the focus is on the UK and the US, other countries like Australia and Canada offer excellent options.

By carefully considering these factors and exploring the universities mentioned above; the student can make an informed decision that aligns with their academic and athletic goals.

Would you like to delve deeper into specific programmes or universities based on the student's preferences?
Citation: https://gemini.google.com/app/e76108ac1de03872; accessed 27/07/2024

This dialogue can continue, and you can add further prompts and suggestions for refinement or a varied response, as needed. A student can do this research on their own, with you or with a parent or guardian. Using LLMs in this way for research allows students to conduct focused and targeted research that pertains to their specific situation. Finding options they are interested in and enthusiastic about can be extremely helpful at the beginning of the process, as it shows students what they are aiming for.

Use of AI for university references

When time is limited, we might be tempted to use GenAI to help write references for students, given that this can be one of the most time-intensive aspects of a teacher or Adviser's job. However, you should be vigilant about sharing data about students with LLMs; our advice would be to avoid giving any data over to an LLM or other platform that could be used to identify individual students. The best advice is to avoid using it for writing references; it is no substitute for your words.

Use of AI for ideas to support your work

GenAI can be used helpfully for organisational tasks and for staff professional development in a number of ways.

Scenario

You have recently been put in charge of the US and international advising element of your careers or Higher Education programme. You have been given one period of dedicated time per fortnight to work with students either as a group or individually.

Suggestions

A LLM such as ChatGPT or Gemini can provide you with the base of a plan. Using the information relevant to your programme, you might use the following prompt:

I have 10 weeks to prepare a cohort of students to make US university applications. I have one hour per fortnight to work with these students. I know that I need to cover the following material within this set of sessions: making a long list of universities, making a short list of universities, filling out the US application form and anything else you think might be relevant.

The LLM will then provide you with a plan that you can use as a base for your own programme with relevant modifications that work within your setting.

Scenario

A Year 12 student has included unusual phrasing in their personal statement: 'a policy for maximizing utility and desirable outcomes' and 'a package of measures to leverage international cooperation'. You suspect that the student has copied and pasted AI-generated text into their personal statement. What is your school/college policy on this? How do you respond?

Suggestions

Your school or college should have a policy on student use of AI; if not, speak to the relevant member of your Senior Leadership Team and ensure that one is written for whole-school use, that includes details about the use of AI for university applications.

For students, the pitfall of using a Large Language Model such as ChatGPT is that it will never sound like them, a 17-year-old; it produces often verbose phrasing or meaningless and generic language. This is why our best advice is not to use it. However, be careful accusing students of using GenAI; equally, do not rely wholesale on websites or programmes that claim to be able to spot AI within student writing as these are often inaccurate. Your student may have used GenAI, or they may have adopted elevated language, believing this is the key to a successful personal statement or US essay.

Ask the student to talk you through their statement and explain it to you. If they are unable to do so and you suspect they have not been wholly truthful about whether they have written the statement or essay themselves, you may want to remind them of any or all of the following: universities expect personal statements and US application essays to be written by the candidate and are attuned to discrepancies between different parts of an application; only you can write in your voice – it is called a personal statement because the student, not anyone else, writes it.

AI and the future of admissions and selection processes

It is unclear at the moment how AI is already being used or might be used in selection processes, both by universities and employers. To speculate too much further would be unhelpful. However, what we can observe currently is that university admissions tests show no signs of going away. As opposed to coursework or writing samples, standardised admissions tests are one of the only ways a university or employer can ensure that the work presented by the student was actually completed by the student. Students who are using GenAI to complete either schoolwork or university application documents should understand this.

Entrance tests of some kind are likely to be required for the foreseeable future, not least because they are proctored tests and cannot be circumvented by a student's use of AI. A number of UK universities cut their applicant pools using scores from various entrance tests. Students coming to UK universities from the US or other systems that do not use GCSEs/A levels/the IB are likely to not only be required to take entrance exams required by the universities but also to present Advanced Placement exam scores (tests that are administered by the US-based College Board) as well. In US admissions, standardised testing requirements (either the SAT or ACT) have been reinstated at highly selective institutions, and testing will likely continue to be required for admission there for the foreseeable future.

According to an Institute of Student Employers (ISE) survey (450 members) *'48% are planning to use more sophisticated way to screen out applicants'*, suggesting that the role of machines will become more important.

Useful links

- Khanmigo: Khan Academy's AI-powered teaching assistant and tutor https://khanmigo.ai/
- Russell Group policy on AI https://russellgroup.ac.uk/news/new-principles-on-use-of-ai-in-education/
- University of Cambridge advice for undergraduates https://www.cam.ac.uk/stories/ai-and-scholarship-manifesto
- https://www.undergraduate.study.cam.ac.uk/apply/ai-and-undergraduate-applications
- Yale admissions podcast https://yaledailynews.com/blog/2023/09/18/admissions-office-sidesteps-formal-ai-policy-refers-applicants-to-podcast

Looking ahead: Key takeaways and questions to consider

- *Staff.* **No machine can replicate a human voice; students should write without the assistance of AI.** How will you develop and update your school or college policy on student use of AI?

- *Students.* **Universities want to read essays, supplements and personal statements written by the student, and AI should be avoided as it is likely to constitute academic malpractice.** How can you create opportunities for students to practice using their own voices to create compelling application materials without resorting to AI?

Conclusion

Our aim has been to discuss how to support students with their post-18 options, focusing in particular on university applications. Our book has focused on traditional institutional routes and in-person schools, which are relevant to the vast majority of settings, though, of course, this may not be the case everywhere. In some schools, there will be a bias towards academic routes and university entry; in others, there may be a bias towards going straight into employment. It is an exciting task to create, develop and maintain a CEIAG programme that will help your students evaluate all of their options and think beyond the well-trodden routes. Inevitably, in any school or college context, there may be a perception of the 'correct' path students should take based on the 'normal' routes and trends for past cohorts. Your task is to support students within your context but also to challenge preconceived notions of what students should do when they leave school. In some settings, you might want to increase your students' awareness of UK, US and international universities, and we explored how to set up and establish these programmes.

The digital revolution has brought about a revolution in employment, education and learning, and this means that new jobs and streams of income are constantly evolving. What is considered a 'suitable choice' depends on multiple factors: educational, social and cultural. While university and employer outreach programmes might raise awareness and interest in a particular academic or vocational route, there is no substitute for creating a school or college environment where students become prepared for deciding what the best route for them to pursue is, whether university study, training or employment.

The purpose of this book has been to help you support your students as best as you can. If you are involved in advising students with their post-18+ choices, university applications or Careers guidance, you play a crucial and vitally important role.

These are some of the key points for schools and colleges:

- **The role of your school or college.** This plays an important role in various ways:
    - with resourcing and developing staff who can advise students;
    - with producing documents and references to support their applications;

- with preparing students with the knowledge and skills needed for the successful transition from school to university, employment, training or apprenticeships.
- **Context.** Understand your context in terms of the needs of students, their parents and your colleagues. Students should make their own informed choices about what they will do next. Our task as educators is to help students achieve their potential while they are our responsibility at school and college. In Chapter 2, we explored how you can help them increase their chances of successful applications.
- **Students.** Be responsive to the students; they are always at the forefront of your work.
- **Staffing.** Provide appropriate levels of resources for staff with expertise and time.
- **Advising.** Encourage students to pursue something suitable that they will enjoy. Your school or college can advise, encourage and support them, but students must 'drive the application process' and make their own informed choices.
- **University applications.** Going to university is part of a student's intellectual journey and personal growth. We suggested ideas in Chapters 5 and 8 to set up programmes to help them navigate their UK, US and international university options.
- **Transition.** It is one thing for a student to gain a place; it is another thing for them to succeed and finish. Schools need to develop curriculums so students acquire the skills they need to flourish while at university or in a job. Schools need to promote mental health, resilience and personal development so students can cope with setbacks.
- **Change in the sector is ongoing.**
    - Students are increasingly aware of global opportunities, whether that means full-time study in another country for their entire degree or short-term study outside their UK institution.
    - Funding models within British universities are likely to change sooner rather than later. Will this lead students to turn away from traditional university routes or encourage them to look beyond traditional three- and four-year courses in the UK?
    - While AI presents a new challenge for schools and universities in terms of academic honesty and the authenticity of student writing, student voice and student writing are here to stay.

What you do is vital, and we hope that the information in this book will help you to create a thriving and exciting strategy to support your students.

Recommended reading

HEAP 2026: University Degree Course Offers by Brian Heap.
Who Gets in and Why: A Year inside College Admissions by Jeffrey J. Selingo, Sean Patrick Hopkins, et al.
Colleges That Change Lives: 40 Schools That Will Change the Way You Think about College by Loren Pope, Hilary Masell Oswald.
The Anxious Generation: How the Great Rewiring of Childhood Is Causing an Epidemic of Mental Illness by Jonathan Haidt.
The Gatekeepers: Inside the Admissions Process of a Premier College by Jacques Steinberg.
The 100-Year Life: Living and Working in an Age of Longevity by Lynda Gratton & Andrew Scott.
The Future of the Professions: How Technology Will Transform the Work of Human Experts by Richard Susskind and Daniel Susskind.
The Fourth Education Revolution: Will Artificial Intelligence Liberate or Infantilise Humanity? by Sir Anthony Seldon and Oladimeji Abidoye.

www.ingramcontent.com/pod-product-compliance
Lightning Source LLC
Chambersburg PA
CBHW041437300426
44114CB00025B/2911